MURDER
at
Matfield Green

JIM NORTON

Copyright 2025 by Jim Norton
This book is a production of Gold Badge Writing.

All right reserved. No part of this publication may be reproduced, copied, stored, or transmitted in any form or by any means electronic, mechanical, scanned, photocopied or otherwise without the express written permission from the publisher. It is unlawful to copy or post any portion onto a website or other means of display, without permission from Janine Chellington Press.

Janine Chellington Press
ISBN: 979-8-9906048-7-2

Disclaimer: Use of Names, Graphic Content, and Ethical Considerations
This book contains real names, locations, and entities, unless otherwise noted. Every effort has been made to present factual and accurate information. Any errors or misstatements are entirely unintentional and are not intended to defame, slander, or cause harm to any person or organization.

The narrative includes graphic depictions of real-life incidents that reflect the challenges faced by law enforcement. These descriptions are presented to offer an authentic and respectful portrayal of the complexities encountered in the line of duty. Reader discretion is advised, as some content may be emotionally intense or distressing. Readers are encouraged to practice self-care as needed.

To maintain ethical standards, the author has deliberately excluded personal anecdotes or details that could compromise operational security, trade secrets, or sensitive law enforcement methodologies. This decision reflects a commitment to preserving the integrity and confidentiality of law enforcement practices.

Permission was sought and obtained from individuals named in this book, where applicable. The author has taken great care to respect the privacy and rights of all persons involved, reinforcing a responsible and ethical approach to storytelling. Those named have been taken from public sources including but not limited to public records and news outlets.

This book does not intend to glorify, sensationalize, or promote illegal or unethical behavior. Its purpose is to provide a balanced and truthful account of real-life events while honoring legal and moral boundaries.

By continuing to read, you acknowledge and accept the terms of this disclaimer and understand that the stories within depict complex and often challenging realities.

"We make a living by what we get, we make a life by what we give."

Winston Churchill

Trooper Conroy O'Brien
END OF WATCH MAY 24, 1978

Introduction

This story is special to me for more reasons than merely a desire to tell you about Conroy O'Brien. You see, on the day after the murder of Trooper Conroy O'Brien, I was a thirteen-year-old kid. I was in deep mourning—utterly grief stricken, because my dad had passed away two months prior. My dad, Sgt. Bobby Lee Norton was a 20-year veteran of the Kansas State Highway Patrol.

While sitting at the kitchen table with my mother, the doorbell rang. I hurried to open the door. Standing on our front porch, waiting to chat with my mom, stood Kansas Highway Patrol Trooper Charlie Smith—he was my dad's best friend. As a young boy, I loved being around Charlie. He was one of my father's most valued troopers, and he was like a superhero to me. Charlie was comical and brought joy to my world. I remember my mom, who was also in mourning over the loss of my dad, walking up to Charlie, hugging him and telling him how happy she was to see him alive and well. Just the day before, Charlie had been involved in an intense shootout with Jimmie K. Nelms, Walter Myrick and Stanford Swain, who had been involved in killing Conroy O'Brien. Nelms had also come very close to killing Charlie, too.

I will forever remember Charlie sitting at our dining room table describing the events that had unfolded the day before. As I sat at the table, frozen, I listened to the graphic details Charlie described to Mom and me about his shootout. Charlie helped me visualize he had not gotten his first cup of coffee, his mouth still dry with sleep, when he passed by the suspects who police were seeking for the death of his brother in blue. Charlie described his chase of the suspects into a field and how he had to crash his car into the bad guy's vehicle.

In that moment, Charlie relived and relayed the event of the suspect ramming into his front bumper and how the driver started firing his handgun from the open window, just feet away. To this day, I can still see the look on his face as he told us that if he were right-handed, he would be dead. The look on his face was a mixture of horror, satisfaction and pure relief, all displayed as one.

Charlie described how the bullets started flying through his windshield toward his head and how, as he leaned to his right to get below the dashboard, he could reach his holster on his left hip to grab his gun. Charlie said he fired back and how the gun battle between the driver, passenger and himself plowed forward. The story was fascinating to the thirteen-year-old version of myself.

I remember feeling admiration that my childhood hero had won this important battle and caught the bad guys.

As Charlie finished telling his story, I remember walking to our driveway and looking at Charlie's shot-up patrol car.

Remembering the damage of bullet holes in his patrol car's windshield—those punctured holes directly in front of the steering wheel. Bullet holes had also punctured the driver's door. As a young boy, it seemed exciting to see something like that, yet scary to see that someone I looked up to could have died. To this day, it feels surreal to think I was so fortunate to have had that experience with Charlie in May 1978.

There are certain people who come into your life who are so special you do not realize how lucky you were to have known them until they are gone. Such a person in my childhood was Trooper Charlie Smith. I also know my father would have beamed with pride at Charlie's heroic acts.

Table of Contents

1: A Kansas Kid
2: The Kansas Highway Patrol
3: The Start of the Family.
4: The Beginning of the End
5: Matfield Green
6: The Last Stop
7: An Act You Can Not Take Back
8. The Shootout
9: The Search for a Killer
10: The Autopsy and Dr. Thomas Noguchi
11: A Wife's Grief
12: Let's Make a Deal
13: The Trial
14: The Appeal
15: The Reply
16: Walter Myrick's Story
17: The Prison Sentences
18: Contact with a Murderer
19: The Highway
20: A Father's Love
Afterward from the Author
Acknowledgments

1: A KANSAS KID

Small towns are special places. A small town is more than just a dot on the map—it is a way of life. It is where kids ride bikes freely down quiet streets, where people leave their doors unlocked, not out of carelessness, but trust. Crime is rare, and the sense of community is strong. With fewer than 1,500 people, chances are, if you stay a while, you will know nearly everyone. You will know what they drive, where they work, and the names of their children.

Small towns are tighter-knit than any city or large town could hope to be. Only someone from a small community can completely understand it. In these towns, neighborliness is not just a value. It is a way of living. Because small Kansas towns welcome friendships and a feeling of togetherness, it brings happiness. When tragedy strikes in a small town, neighbors and friends feel the tragedy as if it happened to themselves. They circle their wagons with love, friendship and a genuine sense of caring.

Many Kansas towns have a local hero.

A few examples include:

- Abilene had a son named Dwight D. Eisenhower, who helped win a war and became the 34th President of the United States.

- Russell had a son named Bob Dole, who became a long-term politician in Washington, D.C.

- Atchison had a daughter named Amelia Earhart, who was a pioneer in the aviation world.

- Chapman had a son named Joe Engle, who became an astronaut.

In this story, the small town of Abbyville had a son named Conroy O'Brien, who was artistic, athletic and a wonderful human being, who grew up to become a Kansas Highway Patrolman.

JAMES O'BRIEN

THELMA CADE

Conroy's Parents

Conroy's father, James O'Brien, was born in Oklahoma, the son of a skilled stonemason. He grew up in Las Animas, Colorado, a town built by railroads, hard work and the silent strength of families who started with nothing. Conroy's grandfather, Michael J. O'Brien, had been born in New Mexico and served as a second lieutenant in Arizona's 13th Infantry, stationed on special duty at Fort Elliott, Texas. His wife, Mary Richardson, came from Texas.

James married Helen Maher in Pueblo, Colorado and the couple eventually settled in Hutchinson, Kansas, where they raised a bustling household. Their family grew quickly—fifteen children in all. One child died in infancy and another in a tragic accident, yet the O'Briens pressed on.

For most of his working life, James labored in the Carey Salt Mine, one of Hutchinson's defining industries. Carey Salt was a cornerstone of the city's economy and the reason Hutchinson earned its nickname, "Salt City." The mine's tunnels stretch deep beneath the Kansas plains, where men like James spent long hours in dim light and choking dust, hauling out blocks of pure rock salt. It was exhausting, often dangerous work—marked by the constant rumble of machinery, the sting of brine in the air, and the ever-present risk of injury. Yet for many families, the Carey Salt Mine offered steady employment and a lifeline through hard times.

Around 1922, that danger caught up with James. A work accident cost him his hand. For most, such a loss might have ended a career, but James refused to be undone by misfortune. Instead, he redirected his mechanical curiosity toward invention. In 1924, he designed a new wagon he named the "Jim Coaster," which he patented the following year. In an interview with *The Hutchinson News*, James explained that the wagon's design featured wheels that turned in opposite directions—front and back—making it nearly impossible to tip over. It was a clever innovation, born from both necessity and ambition. A way to earn residual income to support a large family.

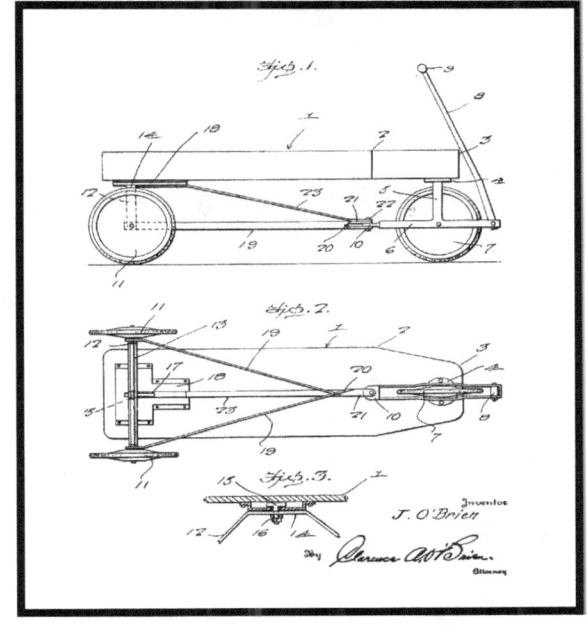

James O'Brien's patent for "Jim's Coaster," 1925. U.S. Patent Office.

The O'Brien's became familiar faces in the local papers, often noted for their large household and occasional milestones. In 1935, *The Hutchinson News* featured them again when Helen gave birth to the city's first baby of the new year. But the years brought their share of strain, and in 1946, James and Helen divorced after more than two decades of marriage.

In the late 1940s, James reaching his 60s, reinvented himself once more. He got his chauffeur's license and began driving for Yellow Cab in Hutchinson. It was there that he met Thelma Cade, a young woman in her twenties who worked as a stenographer for the Meriden Creamery on Main Street. Thelma lived in nearby Abbyville, a small town tucked in the heart of Reno County. Despite their age difference, the two shared a mutual respect and affection that led to marriage and the birth of two children, including Conroy.

When James O'Brien died at seventy-six, Conroy was not yet thirteen. Though still a boy, he carried with him the legacy of a father whose life embodied resilience and quiet perseverance.

Conroy's Childhood

Conroy O'Brien with his mother, Thelma.

    Conroy's hometown of Abbyville is a close-knit community tucked away in the flat, south-central Kansas countryside of Reno County, Kansas. Out of necessity, communities like Abbyville collaborate with other small towns to share educational resources. Students from surrounding small communities attended Fairfield High School in Langdon, Kansas. The local community often comes together on fall Friday nights to support the Fairfield Falcons in hopes of a win. Among the victorious boys celebrated in this story was Conroy O'Brien.

    Conroy always stood out in a crowd. At 6'3" tall in high school, Conroy never used his height to intimidate anyone. Known for his kindness, he never judged people based on their backgrounds. Conroy perfectly reflected his family's values and the small-town life he knew.

During his middle school years, his football coach, Jerry Tomlinson, nicknamed him "Big C." Conroy loved playing football and would lead the charge for the USD 310 Fairfield Falcons. When Conroy's Coach Tomlinson, came under public scrutiny, the young Conroy did not remain silent. Instead, he took to his pen and wrote a letter to the local newspaper in defense of the man he respected. His words revealed a wisdom well beyond his years—a quiet maturity rooted in empathy and faith. Conroy encouraged his community to resist passing judgment on others, reminding them that true understanding comes only through compassion and patience.

Conroy closed his opinion piece with the weight of scripture:
> Until they do have the opportunity to really know and understand him, I hope they quit talking and open their Bibles and read Matthew 7:1.

The verse reads simply yet profoundly:
"Judge not, that ye be not judged." — Matthew 7:1, KJV

Conroy's words struck a chord. A family friend and teacher, Jim Kellerman, wrote to him shortly after the letter's publication. His note (March 1, 1966), Kellerman praised Conroy's courage and character:
> You may be only an 8th grader, but in my books you're a 'big man.' I'm sure your mother must be very proud of you, and some of the Abbyville 'fans' must feel pretty small. Congratulations to you for speaking out!

Conroy showed not only conviction but compassion—the ability to stand for what was right without condemning others. It was a lesson he seemed to understand instinctively: that kindness and understanding, not judgment, are the truest measures of a person's character.

As an eighth grader, Conroy would hang out with his younger brother, Kelvin, and their friend Jim Strong, who were fifth graders. The O'Briens and the Strongs lived three blocks away from each other. The boys often played baseball and football together at the park. Jim felt Conroy was more of a brother than a fellow neighbor kid, because Conroy was always so good to him. As Jim reflected on their shared childhood, saying "Conroy never looked down at me for being so much younger. Conroy just liked people and treated everyone as he was supposed to." It was a sentiment felt by everyone who knew him. When the boys entered high school, Conroy's personality never changed. As a senior, Conroy did not allow his senior rank to go to his head. He still treated both Kelvin and Jim as his brothers.

Attending a small high school affords the opportunity to be involved in multiple sports and activities. Throughout his high school days, he was an active member of the student council. During this time, he and his fellow student council members teamed up with the debate squad, who challenged the local school board, ending in successfully getting a vending machine at the school for after-school snacks. His athleticism on the basketball court and football field, and his musical talent in the band, made him a well-rounded student. He also wrote sports articles for the high school paper and was active in Hi-Y, a YMCA youth organization. During his senior year, he became student body president and earned a football scholarship to Sterling College.

Fairfield High School Falcons, Football Team. Langdon, Kansas. 1968-1969. Conroy O'Brien, #83 pictured front row, second from right.

Conroy O'Brien, Student Council, Fairfield High School 1968-1969.

Fairfield High School Falcons, Basketball Team. Langdon, Kansas. 1968-1969. Conroy O'Brien, #51 pictured second from right.

Fairfield High School Falcons, Track Team. Langdon, Kansas. 1968-1969. Conroy O'Brien, pictured back row, second from left, next to Coach Brooks.

Top: Conroy's Freshman Team, 1970-1971. Conroy pictured, left side, fourth row, wearing a dark jersey, #78.
Center: Sterling College football roster, 1971-1972.
Bottom: Conroy's Sophomore Team, 1971-1972. Pictured standing between #67 and #86. Courtesy of Sterling College from yearbooks, 1971 and 1972.

While at Sterling College, he became an offensive lineman for the football team. Sporting the number 78 on his jersey, Conroy would dominate for two seasons, blocking for the Sterling Knights. Conroy, although seeing things differently than some people do, wanted a more serene life. His views on life were like looking out of a spotless glass window, offering crystal-clear clarity, rather than a dirty one, smudged with grime.

Conroy's initial goal was to earn an art degree. As a visual person, he enjoyed making things with his hands. Enrolling in multiple art courses, he received training in many art forms. For example, in pottery class, he loved getting his hands covered in muddy clay water while spinning the pot on the wheel. He also enjoyed drawing, painting and macrame.

After his two years at Sterling College, he set out as an adult in need of a good job. Conroy scoured the help-wanted ads and found a full-time position at The Coleman Company. The Coleman Company was a large manufacturing and sales company, which made most of its own products. Consisting of outdoor gear and camping supplies, the company's business is in downtown Wichita, Kansas. Conroy was just one piece of a much larger pie, which kept the doors open and the products stocked on the shelves. While working at Coleman, Conroy enrolled at Wichita State University, working towards a bachelor's degree in criminal justice.

In the fall of 1972, Conroy entered a new chapter of his life, and he would find it one weekend returning to his hometown during homecoming weekend. Unbeknownst to Conroy, he would meet someone new who would change his life forever. The DJ's booming music swept up even the shyest kids at the homecoming dance, and they danced with friends, dates or crushes. As the music played, Conroy spotted an unknown girl across the dance floor.

This unfamiliar face belonged to a girl named Tanda. Krista Lee, an alumna of Fairfield High had invited her college friend, a young lady named Tanda Parnell. They both attended Dodge City's Cosmetology School. As the songs played and the youth danced, Tanda peered across the dance floor, locking eyes with Conroy. The young man's tall, handsome physique captivated her. His gaze captivated her. As she stood staring at him, she thought to herself, "God, he is cute." It was also at that moment Tanda silently told herself, "I am going to marry that man." She did not know how she knew it, but deep in her heart, she knew. Tanda asked her friend about him and found out he had a girlfriend. He was unavailable, and she thought he was off limits.

As the college year continued slipping by, day by day, both Conroy and Tanda went about their lives separately. Winter began turning to spring, and Tanda could not get this guy out of her mind.

In January 1973, Conroy and Tanda's paths crossed again. Her friend Krista Lee officially introduced them, and in no time, Conroy and Tanda began their romance. As the two began dating, neither Conroy nor Tanda were trying to set any kind of speed dating record. In retrospect, Tanda called their early relationship, "a whirlwind unlike any other." Recalling those special times would cast a warm smile upon Tanda's face.

Their second meeting did not actually go so great. Conroy had exceeded his limit on beer at the American Legion and had become intoxicated. Tanda did not write Conroy off completely, despite his acting "like an ass." She wanted another date in another setting, without alcohol.

Tanda recalls that on their actual first date, Conroy left a much better impression. During an interview, she reminisced about their first date, St. Patrick's Day, 1973, which happened in Dodge City, Kansas:

> *It was March 17, 1973, when Conroy took me on our first date. It was wonderful; it was the start of everything...Conroy took me to the theater to see a movie. We saw Up the Sandbox starring Barbra Streisand. Then we went to the Armor Room.*

They marked this special day complete with a few green beers.

After this date, things began happening quickly. Tanda glowingly recalled, "It was April 15, 1973, when Conroy proposed to me. I was so in love." In just three months and one week, this blossoming friendship bloomed into a full life together.

They planned a summer wedding for June 23, 1973, at the First Christian Church in Tanda's hometown of Kinsley, Kansas. The bride stood before her father, a vision of 1970s elegance in a wedding gown of sheer dacron layered over satin, the raised waistline and bishop sleeves echoing the era's romantic flair. A stand-up collar framed her face, while re-embroidered lace and a sheer ruffle lent a pinafore effect that softened her silhouette with vintage charm. A garden hat perched atop her carefully arranged hair. To complete her attire, she held a nosegay of pink roses mixed with white and yellow daisies—a sweet, simple bouquet that mirrored her hopeful heart.

While standing in a quiet room inside the church, her father Otis, however, stood stiffly, his expression unreadable but not warm. As he offered his advice, his tone was steady but clipped, the kind of calm that masked deeper unease. Otis said, "Honey, I need to tell

Tanda and Conroy, Wedding Day. Photograph Courtesy of Tanda O'Brien.

you something about this guy you are about to marry."

Tanda's heart sank as negative thoughts poured into her mind. "Oh, Dad, don't ruin my day, please. I know he's a good man," she replied, as tears started forming in her eyes.

His eyes, though fixed on his daughter, occasionally drifted toward the church doors—as if weighing what was ahead. Otis Parnell was a serious man; however, he was also a jokester. Pulling pranks was something he did as often as he could. His personality was a mixture of funny, yet loving and caring. Otis whispered to Tanda:

> *Honey, this boy you like so much, I like him too. Actually, I love and admire the guy, and I know he is perfect for you. You have my and mom's blessings. Everyone says you are the luckiest girl alive.*

The thought of having her father's blessing upon the marriage was exactly what melted her heart and sealed her fate to Conroy forever. Her frown soon turned to a smile, which beamed across her face. A smile that did not leave until after she fell asleep that night. They were perfect for one another. Both families knew it, and they cheered them on at the reception at the wedding. A ring and a kiss sealed the deal.

On their wedding day, the newlywed couple had a grand total of forty-five dollars between them in their bank accounts. Their honeymoon consisted of a one-night stay in a Wichita hotel, before Conroy headed back to work at The Coleman Company.

Although the couple was not rich, they knew money did not buy happiness. That comes from within. They both knew that you can have no earthly possessions and still be in a state of grace and happiness. That was where Conroy and Tanda found themselves after the wedding.

After the wedding ceremony, the couple needed to find their marital home. After a quick search through the newspaper, they found several small rentals they could afford. The couple first lived in a small one-bedroom duplex in Wichita.

Because Conroy worked the night shift at the Coleman Company, he knew Tanda would have greater peace of mind and increased security with a dog to keep her company in their apartment. So, for Tanda's birthday, he brought home a Great Dane puppy Tanda named Dutchess, who would grow into their family as if she were their own child. And as she grew, she also grew protective of Tanda. However, Dutchess had a slight issue with separation anxiety, at least when left for longer than a few minutes.

Tanda vividly remembers one Saturday evening while she and her dad, Otis, went out to dinner, and as they returned home to the small apartment, they found that Dutchess did not approve of being left out of the festivities. Dutchess had single-handedly ruined the couch cushions, a pair of Tanda's shoes, and their bed pillows. It was clear Dutchess was not happy about being left out. Tanda's dad was furious at Dutchess, as some of the furniture she destroyed was still being paid for by the young couple.

Although not funny even years later, Tanda smiled with fondness and a sense of nostalgia when recounting this story: "The dog had even gone into my closet to go after my shoes."

Dutchess was not all bad, though. She would pay off in a big way on a peaceful weekday morning while Conroy slept after working a long night shift at the Coleman Company. Dutchess noticed something amiss and began barking. Upon checking, Tanda found a window peeper who was peering in on her. As Dutchess barked and growled, wanting to attack, the hair on his spine standing up, and with teeth glistening, Tanda let Dutchess out the side door to chase the window peeper down. The police arrived and captured and arrested the man. Tanda never told Conroy about the window peeper, as she did not want him worrying over her as she knew he would.

It was during this timeframe that Conroy felt the time was right for him to look more downstream into a career, rather than just working a "normal job." Tanda knew Conroy's uncle, Trooper Billie Jo Jones, was the one who put the idea of law enforcement in his mind. She knew Conroy was going for it, full steam ahead.

The early months of 1974 had brought Conroy to a crossroads where he was going to have to decide what he really wanted in life. Because of the criminal justice classes, he decided a career in law enforcement would be a great path to follow. Tanda was completely supportive of his decision. After examining the options, he applied for a job as a Kansas Highway Patrolman. Conroy believed the job would open many opportunities for them as a family. He also believed that being a state trooper would be a fun and exciting career. His uncle, Trooper Billie Jo Jones, shared with him what the position entailed. As he looked up to his uncle, he believed it would be the right career fit for him. However, little did he know just how rigorous the hiring process for the Highway Patrol would be.

On a spring morning, Conroy sat in a large room filled with other hopeful applicants for a two-hour written exam. The exam comprised several hundred multiple-choice, mostly common-sense questions. After passing the written exam, he had to pass a physical exam at the state-approved doctor's office. A psychological test followed by a thorough assessment and a psychiatric interview, which involved written and oral examinations of his mental state. After being found to be of sane mind, the process concluded when KHP (Kansas Highway Patrol) conducted a very thorough background check. The background check process involved gathering opinions of and about Conroy from family, friends and past and present employers. Through the process, doubt began consuming Conroy. Would he complete the process, or was a "thanks, but no thanks" letter in his future? Conroy felt worn out with the hiring process at the Kansas Highway Patrol.

2: THE KANSAS HIGHWAY PATROL

Conroy's wait ended in early September 1974. Being accepted into the Kansas Highway Patrol filled him with joy. He beamed with pride and excitement as he gathered with family to share the exciting news.

Tanda + Conroy

Conroy began his career as a Kansas State Trooper on September 18, 1974. As a young married couple with few possessions to their name, Conroy's old Plymouth Duster being one of those possessions, sharing became the norm for the two. Tanda would have to drive Conroy to Salina to attend the Kansas Highway Patrol Academy. On that fall day so many years ago, Tanda remembers pulling into the parking lot, kissing Conroy goodbye and watching him walk into the building to start his wonderful new career.

Conroy, having already enrolled in his college courses at Wichita State when the KHP academy began, needed help to juggle both school and work. As many people would have put the college courses on hold, Conroy was not like many people. While away at training, Tanda helped him stay current in his classes by attending the Wichita State classes for him, taking notes so he could study her work before he took the tests or wrote his assigned papers. Nowadays, people would probably disallow the methods he employed to pass his college classes, and they might see them as cheating. Their dedication to each other shone through every day.

Without Tanda's help, it would have been extremely difficult, if not impossible, for Conroy to accomplish both a college degree and graduating from the police academy.

In the dead of winter, 1974–1975, Conroy completed his Highway Patrol academy classes. He graduated with 30 other new troopers. The graduation ceremony was held February 15, 1975 inside Kansas Wesleyan University's Shriwise Dining Room. Max Milburn, assistant to the college president at Kansas State University gave the commencement address:

> Your advancement will not be determined by the number of tickets you write, or the number of arrests you make. This is not the way, anymore than it is for a teacher who mistakenly thinks his or her bright future depends upon flunking the most students....You joined a proud outfit today...You have the most to gain by carrying on a its rich traditions by making your full contribution to its future strength and character—and by doing so, strengthening confidence of the people in the government by serving them with professionalism, integrity and compassion.

After graduation, Conroy took his first assignment at a post in Valley Center, Kansas. Tanda frowned at this news. She knew it could have been worse. She was not feeling thrilled about moving out of Wichita. Because of the assignment, they had to leave their cherished new apartment and move into an old, two-story house in Valley Center, a move she very much disliked.

Within a year, they reassigned Conroy back to the Wichita region, and their life became a little easier. Although Tanda described their second living arrangement back in Wichita as "a crappy little duplex." She wished they could have stayed in the nice one they had before they moved to Valley Center. However, after a few months, they would move yet again after finding a nicer place in the suburb of Mulvane, Kansas. This new place was also just down the street from Conroy's training officer and friend, Trooper Alan Bachelor.

Police officers are ordinary people with lives outside of work. They occupy their time with hobbies, as many people do. Conroy's friends were aware of his interest in cards and firearms, but were unaware of Conroy's other artistic hobby—needlepoint art or what you could also describe as latch hook art. Conroy would take a square of needlepoint material using needles of different sizes, he would pull a string through the material, following a pattern until the image he was creating appeared in stunning clarity.

Conroy O'Brien in his Kansas Highway Patrol Uniform. In the background, the Kansas Highway Patrol Training Center in Salina, Kansas. October 1976. Courtesy of the Smoky Hill Museum; Salina Newspaper Archival Collection.

Conroy's athleticism carried into adulthood, as he jogged a mile and a half each evening. Conroy was also a history buff who excelled at trivia—especially sports and history questions. Conroy once shared with fellow Trooper James Mosher his desire to make a meaningful contribution to society.

Conroy was certainly a man of deep faith. He often spent quiet moments alone, reading biographies and his Bible. Conroy had no fear of people judging his religious values. He was a very grounded person. He knew who he was and how he wanted to live life.

Conroy O'Brien at home celebrating is birthday c1975-1978. Photographs in this chapter are courtesy of Tanda O'Brien.

K-108

K-108 was the badge number assigned to Conroy O'Brien. Each officer is given a unique identification number, which serves to distinguish them within the force.

3: THE START OF A FAMILY

I like to use my brain better than my hands, but that can't keep me from refinishing furniture for the baby's room.

—Conroy O'Brien. Friend and brother in blue, Trooper Allen Bachelor told a reporter Conroy said this to him. *Kansas City Times,* May 25, 1978.

As a young married couple, Conroy and Tanda were living life and learning together. Conroy wanted a child, Tanda shared, "Usually it is the woman who first wishes for this, but in our story, it was Conroy who really desired to have a child." Although Tanda was all in on starting a family, she found it heartwarming Conroy desired a baby to expand their family.

By mid-January 1978, Tanda knew almost instantly she was pregnant. As her pregnancy symptoms alerted her, she knew her own body's changes before Conroy would suspect they were expecting. As Tanda told Conroy the news, his reaction was a mixture of fright and delight.

As they began sharing their news with their families and friends, life continued moving quickly. Conroy phoned his grandma Mayree Cade and inquired about his old high chair and baby bed, saying he would need them. This is how he shared his news of expecting a baby. Conroy and Tanda started purchasing items to prepare for the baby. Among the things Conroy purchased was a camera to record memories and a wood-carved dog pull toy.

In early February 1978, Conroy and Tanda drove to Abbyville for dinner with the O'Brien family. Bursting with excitement, the family shared their experiences and gave advice. During the family gathering, no one around the dining table could have guessed that one of them would never meet this new baby, which was on the way.

The weeks and months passed by with Conroy commuting to work and school. Meanwhile, as Tanda's pregnancy progressed, she developed complications. Her doctor discovered she was positive for the Rh factor. When Rh-positive mothers are pregnant with an Rh-negative fetus, and their blood mixes through the umbilical cord, the mother's immune system produces antibodies that attack the baby's red blood cells. Although not completely uncommon, the issues can be catastrophic and can end the pregnancy.

Tanda noticed spotting far too often when using the bathroom, and pains that should not be happening, began happening more often. Doctor visits became a necessity, and the further along Tanda got into her pregnancy, the worse things seemed to get for her and her unborn baby.

Doctors ran tests and completed examinations and became more concerned. They began wondering if she was going to complete the pregnancy before the birth came full circle. Both Conroy and Tanda tried keeping their spirits up during this tough period, as they knew there could be potential issues swirling around the pregnancy.

Conroy prayed daily about the situation. As the couple kept their sanity together through prayer and conversation, Tanda decided the baby girl, the child Conroy so badly wanted, was going to be named Neely. This happened as Tanda sat on her couch watching a movie, and enjoying some quiet time. Tanda had watched the movie, Valley of the Dolls. As she did, she chose the child's name because actress Patty Duke had played a character named Neely O'Hara. Tanda loved the name. So, Neely it had to be. She felt no other name would do for this special baby girl. During a late evening conversation, Conroy jokingly told Tanda he hoped for twins, a girl named Neely and a boy named Newley, after the character from *Gunsmoke*.

In her spare time, Tanda started learning to use the camera she and Conroy had bought. She remembered snapping a photo of Conroy reading *The Death Penalty*, which he was reading as research for a college paper on capital punishment. Little did she know, this would be the last picture she ever took of him.

On the Sunday before Wednesday, May 24, 1978, as the pregnancy continued, with Tanda now five months pregnant, the couple drove to Abbyville for a family dinner and the community's annual rodeo. They visited friends and had a nice dinner with family, where they discussed Tanda's pregnancy. The family could see the concern on the faces of Conroy and Tanda; however, they assured them everything would work out just fine.

During the trip back to Mulvane after the family dinner, while chatting as Conroy drove the highway, Tanda asked Conroy a deep and thoughtful, yet somewhat concerning, question. Honesty being paramount in their marriage, Conroy and Tanda engaged in extensive discussions about everything. Nothing was out of bounds or off the table between them.
Tanda randomly asked, not really knowing why.

"How do you think you will die, when you do die?"

As Conroy drove along the highway back to their Wichita home, he pondered the question before looking at his wife. Without speaking, Conroy simply moved his right hand down to his side as if grabbing his pistol and pointed a finger as if being shot in the side of his head. The conversation ended with no other words needing to be spoken.

They did not know it, but this would be their last visit to Abbyville—the last time Conroy would be there surrounded by his family and hometown friends. This conversation was on a Sunday, and he would be killed 4 days later.

4: THE BEGINNING OF THE END

On Thursday, April 20, 1978, at 9:00 am, business partners Chad Simmons and Patricia "Pat" Spindler arrived at their Fugitt-Guin Fine Jewelers store in Springfield, Missouri's Southern Hills Shopping Center and unlocked the doors. The pair were simply doing what they did every day, trying to operate a successful business. They switched on the lights and deactivated the alarm; as the morning progressed into the afternoon, satisfied customers finished their purchases, contributing to another successful day. Helping customers find exactly what they wanted was a pleasure for them. Whether it was the perfect watch, a diamond ring or necklace for a special family member, the pair were always happy to help the customers they met. They were good at what they did. Business was good, and they ran a professional jewelry business in the heart of one of Missouri's most visited cities.

The jewelry store, which opened in December 1977, was large, with tall ceilings, gold, green and blue carpets, and beautifully polished, long circular display cases reaching from one end of the store to the other. Hundreds of thousands of dollars' worth of rings, bracelets, diamonds, watches, and other assorted fine wearable pieces were on display. The late afternoon would bring heavier traffic into the store, and business would stay steady until closing time at 6:00 pm. Around 5:40 pm, the store's last paying customers, a husband and wife, entered the store, made their purchase, and left just before closing.

At 6:00 pm, Chad Simmons strolled to the front of the store, turned off the open sign and locked the front doors, leaving himself, Pat Spindler and his wife, Susan Simmons inside. A few minutes later, a man described as "nicely dressed," wearing a tan suit, pink shirt and donning a gray wool flattop "driving cap" by the name of Nelms rattled the front doorknob of the jewelry store, finding it locked. Peering through the window, Nelms could see several people still inside. He knocked on the window, asking to come inside to make a quick purchase.

Chad Simmons, always one to be inviting and patient, walked to the front of the store and unlocked the door, inviting the well-dressed man inside for one last sale of the day. Nelms waltzed inside, acting as cool as could be. As he did, Nelms began looking at several delicate pieces of jewelry, finally inquiring about a figurine.

Simmons quoted the figurine prices and found it surprising that Nelms began heading for the exit. So, Simmons promptly followed him, thinking he would lock up after the customer exited.

To Simmons' surprise, Nelms asked, "You don't want anyone hurt, do you?"

"What do you want?" Simmons replied.

"Everything." Nelms replied. As he uttered those words, Nelms pulled a nickel-plated derringer from his jacket, pointed it at Chad Simmons, and directed him and the two women toward the office. Nelms, who soon had the three jewelry clerks under his control, forced Chad to unlock the display cases and ordered his wife Susan and Pat Spindler to fill a white cloth bag with the contents. Each victim would later describe the bag as having black stripes and a zippered top.

Nelms grew increasingly impatient with Chad's slow pace as the robbery unfolded. Changing his tactics, Nelms demanded his hostages go into the office, where he forced Chad to duct tape his wife's hands and feet, making her lie face down on the floor, keeping her out of the way.

Chad and Pat, held at gunpoint, abandoned Susan on the office floor and obeyed orders to return to the display cases and finish the heist. As the heist continued, Nelms pulled a second handgun from his jacket pocket. This second handgun, described as a silver revolver with a six-inch barrel, kept both Nelms' hands occupied.

Nelms, pointing guns at both Chad and Pat, ordered them to clear out nearly all the jewelry from the display cases.

"Fill the bag," Nelms ordered.

After emptying nearly all the valuables from the display cases, Nelms marched the hostage pair back into the office. This time, Chad taped Pat's hands and feet, and then Nelms bound Chad's arms and legs. Nelms then emptied the cash register and placed the cash into his zippered bag. As Chad lay face down on the office floor, he overheard Nelms using a walkie-talkie. Nelms made several transmissions to an unknown accomplice.

Nelms radioed into his walkie-talkie: "Break for the dog,

break for the dog." The radio squelched as he spoke, "Point three, move, point three, move." Moments after the radio transmissions, Nelms slipped out the back door.

Chad waited about five minutes before the three pulled and tore at their bindings. After freeing themselves, Chad called the police, who arrived within minutes. During crime scene processing, investigators bagged eleven pieces of one-inch-wide torn adhesive tape as evidence. The victims, somewhat in shock from the ordeal, were simply glad it was over and they were alive.

Chad reported his losses. The overall loss ranged from as small as seventy-five thousand dollars to as high as two hundred thousand dollars. Only time would tell once the proverbial dust had settled.

Chad, Pat and Susan gave their statements to the police. Chad shared with the police the key detail of the walkie-talkie communications. The police now knew there were at least two participants in the robbery. Nelms' code words were a signal for a get-a-way car to get into position for him to flee.
According to the Springfield News-Leader, this was one of the costliest robberies in Springfield, Missouri's history. The Springfield Police Department had its hands full, solving this case. Often with a robbery of this magnitude, local and state police collaborate to solve the crime as quickly as possible.

Once the story of the crime hit the newspapers, calls flooded the police dispatch center in the hours and days following the robbery. Several people claimed to have seen a man who resembled the composite drawing; however, no one really gave any substantial information about leads. That is, until a nearby J. C. Penney store's security guards told the store manager, Vicki Robinson, about a suspicious white Buick passenger car that had been sitting in the parking lot for several days.

The car had a Missouri tag on it (Y9R-966) and appeared out of place. Vicki notified the police about the car. The tag check revealed someone had stolen the car from Kansas City, Missouri, a week earlier. Inside the car, police found several items of clothing. During the inventory of the car's contents, police discovered a tan, flat-topped wool cap that matched the description of the cap worn by the robbery suspect a week prior. Officer Applegate of the Springfield Police Department conducted the vehicle inventory search and placed the items from the stolen car into evidence.

Shortly after finding the stolen car, Springfield resident Deanna Henderson, having read about the robbery in the paper, called the dispatch center. Henderson told the dispatcher she had been shopping near the jewelry store at the time of the robbery. She recalled noticing something suspicious. As Deanna walked back to her car in the shopping center parking lot, she remembered seeing a white man with a face covering talking into a walkie-talkie. The man was looking around as if wishing to hide. She saw the man rush to a white mid to full-sized car. Then, the man opened the trunk, where another man wearing a cap waited. The man with the cap placed something in the trunk before driving off together.

Detectives from the Springfield Police Department and the Missouri State Police actively sought any further information that anyone could give. From information gleaned through good police work, they identified a suspect who was the man on the other end of the walkie-talkie transmission. The man's name was Morris Judd. Although police reports do not show how Morris Judd became a person of interest to them. What is known: Judd instantly became suspect number one.

The store owners did not recognize Judd's mugshot, leading police to suspect he was not the man who had completed the armed robbery. However, the police had gathered enough evidence to link Morris to the crime. Nineteen days after the robbery, on May 9, 1978, officers executed a search warrant at Judd's Grenada, Mississippi residence. A search by police turned up a significant amount of the stolen jewelry. Promptly, police arrested Morris Judd and hauled him to the police station for an interview.

Although Morris Judd's statement to the police remains undisclosed, his account implicated Nelms as the gunman in the robbery. After Judd's interview, the Springfield, Missouri, Police Department sought an arrest warrant against Nelms. The police simply needed to find Nelms and hopefully locate the rest of the stolen jewelry.

Robbery composite by Springfield Police Department Detective John Smith and Ted Hobson during the investigation. Courtesy of the Springfield Police, Springfield, Missouri.

Springfield Police work the crime scene at Fugitt-Guin Jewelers as pictured in the Springfield Leader Press.

At around the same time Morris Judd was giving up the goods, Nelms was meeting up with a friend of his in Carrollton, Mississippi, by the name of Walter Myrick. The pair stayed around Carrollton and would be in Mississippi for only another week or two. Nelms needed to move some stolen jewelry. Myrick was trying to stay away from the law, knowing he was a wanted felon for missing a court date in Oklahoma.

One problem was neither Myrick nor Nelms owned a car. As a result, Myrick inquired if his friend, a small-time criminal named Laddie Meeks, would let him borrow his vehicle temporarily. Meeks apparently felt comfortable loaning his car to the pair. Little did he know, Myrick and Nelms had no plans of ever returning it.

Nelms heard about Judd's arrest as part of the robbery they had committed and soon left Mississippi. He was uncertain whether Judd would snitch on him. After borrowing Meeks' 1973 Mercury Marquis, Nelms and Myrick fled to Jackson, Georgia to get away from the area.

While in Georgia, Nelms and Myrick made plans to drive westward to Denver, Colorado. It was in Jackson, Georgia where Nelms met a young man named Stanford Swain. It was Swain's older brother who had introduced Swain to Myrick and Nelms. Swain needed a ride to Denver to visit family members and was simply looking for a ride, cheaper than a bus trip would cost. According to Swain's later testimony, he had never met Nelms prior to getting a ride toward Denver. Swain also claimed he was unaware that Nelms had a criminal background or that a warrant for robbery was out for Nelms' arrest. From Georgia, the now trio of Nelms, Myrick and Swain drove west to Tulsa, Oklahoma.

After driving around Tulsa's seedy side, they gassed up Meeks' Mercury, checked a map for the quickest route to Denver and headed out of Tulsa with Nelms at the wheel. They headed west in Oklahoma on US Route-412, toward I-135.

The clock struck midnight.
A new day was beginning: May 24, 1978.
Little did they know it would not be their finest day.

The trio should have been able to arrive in Salina, Kansas in less than five hours after leaving Tulsa. From there, a six-hour drive west on I-70 would take them to Denver. However, during the trip between Tulsa and I-135, Nelms began feeling sleepy and wanted someone else to drive. Somewhere near I-135, Myrick took over driving and Nelms curled up on the back seat for what should have been an uneventful nap.

Neither Myrick nor Swain had ever traveled across Kansas from the south. One could lose their way if they were not paying attention to the road signs. As Myrick drove, the Kansas highway suddenly turned into the Kansas Turnpike and several options appeared like tree branches in front of him. These highway branches appeared south of Wichita, giving little time to choose their path.

Taking I-235 around the west side of Wichita, (which was not what he wanted,) would limit Myrick's options. He could also drive north on I-135 to Salina, which was what he was supposed to have done. However, he took the easterly branch onto the Kansas Turnpike's I-35. Having taken the turnpike, Myrick soon discovered his mistake, realizing within miles that he was on the wrong road. Neither Swain nor Myrick had read their map correctly, or at all.

As Myrick drove the turnpike to the north and east, heading toward Emporia, he could not turn around as there was a center concrete barrier. Myrick soon found he would have to drive to Emporia before he could turn around and correct his error. Myrick sped along as he tried to correct his path.

As time slipped by, minute by minute, the clock had reached 4:45 am. At this witching hour, Myrick saw flashing red lights in his rearview mirror; it was a patrol car. Myrick's heart raced with worry and anticipation. Myrick slowed the Mercury and began pulling to the side of the road. Little did he know, this traffic stop would change his life forever.

5: MATFIELD GREEN

Matfield Green, a small but storied community nestled in the heart of the Flint Hills, carries a quiet legacy shaped by ranching, the railroad and the undisturbed tallgrass prairie. Located in Chase County, they named the town after Matfield, in Suffolk County, England. English settlers came to Kansas in the late 19th century. They officially platted the town in the 1870s, during a time of rapid westward expansion. The surrounding hills and open range drew settlers who saw opportunity in cattle ranching and agriculture, although the thin soil of the Flint Hills proved better suited to grazing than farming.

Matfield, England, is a proud southern countryside European village south of London. "Matfield Green" in Europe is simply a large green park in the center of town. The British call their parks "the green."

The Atchison, Topeka and Santa Fe Railway played a critical role in the Kansas town's development. Matfield Green became a key stop for shipping cattle and supplies when the railroad reached it in the 1870s. Like many prairie towns, the train depot became the hub of activity, bringing in goods, people and news from across the region. The presence of the railroad helped sustain Matfield Green through the early 20th century, even as other small towns faded from the map. The tracks still cut through the town today, part of the BNSF Railway system.

At its peak, Matfield Green had all the marks of a thriving small town: a school, general stores, a post office and a hotel. In the early 1900s, the town had nearly 300 residents. As America modernized, many residents moved to larger cities for economic opportunities. The Dust Bowl, the Great Depression and changes in transportation all contributed to a population decline. Still, the people who remained held onto the town's identity, maintaining its quiet resilience amidst the vast beauty of the Flint Hills.

The installation of the Kansas Turnpike near Matfield Green in the 1950s marked a significant development in both transportation and the region's relationship to the wider state and country. Opened in 1956, the Kansas Turnpike stretches from the Oklahoma border to Kansas City, providing a critical north-south transportation corridor. The section near Matfield Green passes through the Flint Hills, one of the most scenic and ecologically important regions in the state, known for its tallgrass prairie.

While Matfield Green itself is a small, rural community, the construction of the turnpike brought it a rare distinction: it became the site of one of the few service areas along the route. The Matfield Green Service Area, located roughly halfway between Wichita and Emporia, serves motorists with fuel, restrooms and food—offering a vital rest stop in a relatively remote part of the state. Its placement underscores the town's geographic importance, even as its population declined.

The installation of the turnpike was both a blessing and a mixed legacy for Matfield Green. On one hand, it physically connected the region to major cities, enabling easier travel and commerce. On the other hand, the turnpike largely bypassed the town proper, reducing direct traffic into the community itself, which mirrored a broader trend across America where highways contributed to the economic decline of small towns that were once dependent on highway traffic. Still, the nearby service area has helped keep the name Matfield Green visible to thousands of drivers each day. Kansas travelers know Matfield Green as a routine stop.

Importantly, the construction of the Kansas Turnpike through the Flint Hills sparked early conversations about preservation versus progress. Engineers and environmentalists alike were mindful of the unique prairie landscape, and though construction went ahead, it did so with increased awareness of the ecological impact. Today, the Matfield Green area is part of a larger movement to balance infrastructure with conservation, particularly through efforts tied to the Tallgrass Prairie National Preserve and ranching operations that protect native grasses.

In this way, Matfield Green's connection to the Kansas Turnpike tells a broader story—not just of road building, but of how infrastructure intersects with rural identity, environmental stewardship and the passage of time. While the town remains small, its name endures on turnpike signs and maps, a quiet landmark amid the vast Flint Hills landscape.

Recently, Matfield Green experienced a cultural revival

of sorts. The town attracted artists, conservationists, and those seeking a slower pace of life connected to the land. The surrounding prairie—home to the Tallgrass Prairie National Preserve just north of town—has gained national attention for its ecological importance. This connection to preservation and the arts has breathed new life into the town, even if the population remains small.

6: THE LAST STOP

To balance work, school and his personal life, Conroy worked a full-time night shift as a Kansas State Highway Patrol Trooper. This freed him up during the day to attend his classes at Wichita State University. As a Criminal Justice major, he hoped someday to join the FBI. To accomplish his goal, Conroy needed to make it easier for himself and Tanda while he completed his degree.

To accomplish the full-time work, college degree and happy home life, Conroy had to avoid rotating shifts, which most troopers worked. To help move his college along, he had to transfer to the Kansas Highway Patrol's Turnpike Authority-Division (KHP TA). The turnpike troopers worked set shifts. Conroy knew the transfer would allow him to work the late-night shift. If he could transfer to KHP TA, he would work the midnight shift, and he could take his classes during the day. This was a sacrifice he was willing to make.

Kansas has only one turnpike. It is a 236-mile-long, controlled-access toll road that runs in a general southwest/northeast direction from the center of the Kansas/Oklahoma border, north and east to Topeka. The turnpike passes through several major Kansas cities, including Wichita, El Dorado and Emporia, before ending near Kansas City.

Conroy filled out the forms to make his transfer request. He had to wait a few months before he received the good news that they had granted his transfer.

In 1977, Conroy was ready to move forward with the new assignment. Conroy had no desire to move out of the Wichita region and with a bit of luck, received his assignment to the same region of Kansas he had already been working; it simply moved him from patrolling the county and state roads solely to the turnpike.

After the transfer, Conroy began his journey of working the night shift and taking college classes during the day. This left little time for sleep, however, for Conroy, a young man of twenty-six years, with four years of highway patrol experience under his belt. He felt well-equipped to handle this short-term inconvenience.

The assignment to the turnpike was not much different from his earlier assignment of patrolling Sedgwick and Butler Counties looking for speeders or citizens in need of assistance. To him, the turnpike assignment would probably someday become mundane.

but the payoff of finishing his college degree was something he was willing to trade for having to see the same stretch of highway day after day.

KHP assigned numerous troopers to the Kansas Turnpike. However, Conroy was the only trooper patrolling the 90 miles stretch between Emporia and Wichita during the late hours of May 23, 1978. Conroy's shift began on Tuesday, May 23, 1978, just minutes before 11:00 pm.

Stepping over to his beautiful wife as she sat on the couch, Conroy gave Tanda a goodbye kiss before opening his front door and taking the short walk to his patrol car. Tanda sat admiring her husband in his freshly pressed light blue highway patrol uniform, with the pristine light blue stripe running down the side of his dark blue trouser leg, his boots shined to a glisten and his gun belt gleaming, her eyes filled with pride. Little did she know it would be the last time Conroy would stroll from their home. This last goodbye kiss they shared would linger in her mind.

After leaving his house to begin his night shift, Conroy first needed to drive to the Turnpike Headquarters, where he was being issued a brand-new bullet-proof vest. The vest was tailor-made to his exact measurements. It would become part of his standard uniform from the moment he put it on.

After arriving at headquarters, Conroy removed his uniform shirt, he slipped the ballistic vest over his head, tightening the Velcro straps to secure it in place. Slipping his backup pistol and shoulder holster in place came next, followed by his uniform shirt. Conroy was fifteen minutes away from starting a shift that would have long-lasting consequences for many people to come.

To Conroy, it was just another quiet, midweek-night shift. Traffic was light, and the weather was perfect, with a low of 65, topping out at 85 degrees. Conroy looked forward to the night shift ahead. However, little did he know it would be his last.

Conroy's last radio communication to dispatch was at 4:08 am, just before he helped a traveler locate I-70. He logged a motorist assist and called "10-8," meaning "I'm on duty and ready to respond to calls," to the dispatcher at 4:15 am.

At 4:22 am, Conroy stopped a car for speeding and issued a ticket for 75-mph in a 55-mph zone. He was back in service at 4:30 am; however; he did not call this traffic stop out over his radio.

At around 4:45 am, while Conroy was monitoring traffic near the small town of Matfield Green, he spotted a Mercury vehicle traveling north toward Emporia. Conroy checked the vehicle's speed, traveling 63-mph in the 55-mph zone. Conroy pursued the car to initiate a traffic stop.

Conroy, although a fantastic human being and a diligent, hardworking state trooper, was not perfect, and he made mistakes, just as everyone does. Despite being a relatively minor oversight, he again failed to follow protocol and inform the dispatcher he had made a traffic stop. This was two stops in a row he had failed to call in for.

Conroy failed to call out his stop location or give the make, model or tag number of the car to his dispatcher. Nor did he radio dispatch and run the driver's license of the person he had stopped. Although somewhat unusual, officers have done the same many times, and doing so is often not a big deal. No one will ever know why Conroy felt justified in not notifying dispatch. Turning on his rotating red light to stop the car, Conroy pulled behind the speeder but got no response from the driver. As the Mercury continued northbound, Conroy initiated his siren, signaling the car to stop and pull over. As the siren yelped, the driver slowed and finally pulled to the side of the road near mile marker 94.5.

Railroad workers Charles Little and William Meyers, who were working half a mile from the traffic stop, verified this location. Charles Little later told investigators he had seen the patrol cars' red lights come on and heard the siren honk during what he perceived was a traffic stop. After seeing the stop occur, he returned to his work, and never heard another noise from the location of the patrol car. Meyers had been inside a brick switch house and had not witnessed the traffic stop.

As the driver, Myrick pulled to the side of the road and stopped along the east ditch. He woke his passengers, Nelms and Swain, so they knew a cop was stopping them. The beige 1973 Mercury

Marquis four-door rolled to a stop with Conroy's red light flashing in its rearview mirror.

Conroy pulled his car behind the Mercury and put his patrol car in park, opened his driver's door, put his left foot on the ground and stepped out of his patrol car. He gently and with perfect placement, sat his trooper hat on his head and walked up to the last car stop he would ever make. Just two miles outside of the small town of Matfield Green, the future for so many was about to change forever.

7: An Act You Cannot Take Back

Approaching the driver during a traffic stop is just a daily fact of life for a police officer. In a brief period, an officer assesses the situation and decides how they will proceed. During the first thirty seconds, an officer decides whether they should ask the driver to remain in their car or exit. It is all about safety at this point of the stop. It is also this same thirty seconds that the officer forms an opinion if they will make an arrest or not.

The air was crisp yet humid, making the days feel more like summer than spring. Conroy exited his patrol car, yet never made it to the driver's window. Instead, the speeding driver, Walter Myrick, from Mississippi, exited his car on his own, and they met at the trunk of the Mercury.

This was not ideal for Conroy, as he should have ordered the driver to return to the car. According to the KBI (Kansas Bureau of Investigation) case file, Myrick politely asked what the problem was. Myrick told Conroy he did not have his driver's license with him and identified himself as Tommy McClendon. Conroy decided it would be best to have Mr. Tommy McClendon (Myrick) come sit in his patrol car so they could chat. Apparently, he felt doing so was the safest method while they worked through the process of issuing a traffic ticket. Although no one can see into the future, allowing Myrick to exit the Mercury was a catastrophic tactical error on Conroy's part.

Myrick did not act hostile or try to fight Conroy. Everything seemed normal in Conroy's mind. He was just doing what cops do, dealing with the public in a professional manner. Moments later, Myrick walked to the front passenger door of Conroy's patrol car, where he took a seat inside. After walking Myrick to the passenger seat of the patrol car, Conroy joined him in the driver's seat. It was there that Conroy removed his trooper hat and placed it on the dashboard, directly in front of him.

During their initial discussion, Myrick informed Conroy he had borrowed the vehicle from a friend and was on his way to Denver, however, he had taken a wrong turn in Wichita and mistakenly gotten onto the turnpike, instead of staying on I-135 toward Salina. (*Had Myrick not made this mistake, he would have followed I-135 north and turned west onto I-70, toward Denver, and this stop would never have happened.)*

Conroy had almost completed filling out a speeding ticket in the name of Tommy McClendon, listing his date of birth as September 17, 1952, which was Myrick's actual date of birth. This would be the last drop of ink Conroy would ever write in his ticket book before everything would change. While filling out the ticket, Conroy's concentration was primarily on what was occurring inside his patrol car. With full darkness still set outside, short of his headlights and his rear flashers, the activity within the Mercury occurred mostly out of Conroy's view.

It was during the time Conroy dealt with Myrick that Nelms, who was sleeping in the back seat, awoke. After waking and seeing the cop car behind them, Nelms became instantly panicked and overly nervous. After hearing about Judd's arrest, Nelms knew the police wanted him for the jewelry store robbery. These suspicions lingered in Nelms' mind; he was absolutely certain he was minutes away from spending years of his life in prison for his crimes.

In fact, Springfield, Missouri, had issued a warrant for Nelms' arrest. However, he did not know this for certain. The fact was, Conroy was unaware he was dealing with a car full of armed felons.

Nelms became frantic as his nerves spiked as if on fire. He was sure he was about to be arrested, when in fact he would not be. It was 1978, and the National Crime Information Center (NCIC) did not have instant checks as it does today. Had Nelms remained in the back seat of the car, all three men would have been on their way in less than five minutes and it would have been hours, if not days before Conroy ever found out he had a carload of criminals in front of him.

Not knowing this, Nelms began freaking out, deciding what he had to do to escape arrest. Swain, sitting in the front seat, did nothing to help calm Nelms' nerves, nor did he try to intervene in whatever Nelms was contemplating. Within seconds of realizing the peril he was possibly in, Nelms decided he had to kill Trooper O'Brien. Swain would later testify about those few seconds while in the Mercury with Nelms. The Kansas Supreme Court document recorded his testimony.

According to Swain, "Nelms retrieved a handgun from the glove box and told Swain, I'm going to kill that mother fucker."

The twenty-one-year-old Swain, ten years Nelms' junior, was afraid of Nelms. Swain also saw the insane look in Nelms' eyes. It was clear to Swain that Nelms had murder on his mind. When Swain failed to act or stop Nelms from retrieving the pistol, everyone's lives changed. This was the first act that Swain could not take back.

Nelms slowly opened the rear passenger door of the Mercury, crouched as he shuffled toward the patrol car, where Conroy sat behind the steering wheel, his concentration set on Myrick. Because Conroy had sat his uniform hat on the dashboard directly in front of him, it obstructed his view out the windshield. He never saw Nelms approach his car. Because of this, Nelms easily surprised Conroy as he snuck up to the passenger door. Once Conroy spotted Nelms, for some unknown reason, he told Nelms to come to the driver's door to speak with him. As Nelms reached the driver's door, Nelms pounced and pointed his handgun directly at Conroy's face. Nelms screamed at Conroy to keep his hands in sight and ordered Conroy out of the car. Being caught off guard, Conroy was now at a huge disadvantage. Conroy had just become a hostage.

After getting full control of Conroy, Nelms ordered him out of his car, where he removed Conroy's Smith and Wesson Model 19 revolver from its holster and ordered him into the ditch toward the rear of the patrol car. Nelms, with the revolver pointed at Conroy's head, repeatedly ordered him to keep his hands raised and move toward the ditch. Conroy, in a state of panic and desperation, told Nelms, "You don't have to do this," and begged him to stop.

As Conroy stood in the ditch, nearly sixty feet from his patrol car, with his hand upward toward the sky, Nelms swung the revolver at the back of Conroy's head with such force the blow knocked Conroy to his knees. Myrick stood beside Nelms during this assault and did nothing to stop Nelms' assault against Conroy.

Conroy lay stunned and dazed as he knelt in the grass in the middle of the ditch. Still conscious, he begged one final time, telling Nelms, "please don't do this to me." Without any hesitation, Nelms fired two shots from Conroy's .357 revolver into the left side of

Conroy's head, killing him instantly. The first bullet struck Conroy in the center of his left ear. While Conroy lay dead on the grass, the second bullet struck just behind his left ear. Conroy probably never even heard the first shot from the gun going off. Conroy's dead body lay in the ditch, his face downward with his arms bent above his head and his hands lying one on each side of his head. Since Conroy's new bulletproof vest did not shield his head, it unfortunately could not save him.

This was the final act, which Nelms could never take back.

Later, during the investigation, as they transported Conroy's body to the hospital, the KBI learned he had a small semi-automatic, Colt brand, backup pistol hidden in a shoulder holster, under his uniform shirt. Why he did not go for the gun, we will never know. He probably never had the opportunity.

As Conroy O'Brien lay dead in the grass, a panicked Myrick and Nelms hurried to the Mercury. Prior to doing so, Myrick grabbed the ticket book from the patrol car. As they got to the Mercury, Nelms ordered Swain to use a towel and wipe down any trace of fingerprints. Swain went to the patrol car and did as he was told. As soon as Swain got back to the Mercury, the trio fled north on the turnpike.

Little did they know, a motorist had driven past the vehicle stop as Conroy was standing outside with Myrick. The motorist had made a mental note of the car being stopped. Although not exact, the description later given to the patrol would help with finding the criminals as they fled. From the vehicle description given by the witness, the patrol knew the suspect would travel in a large, light colored Cadillac style vehicle.

At 6:00 am, having heard no radio traffic from Conroy since his last radio call at 4:08 am, the Kansas Highway Patrol dispatch radioed him for a safety check. As silence hung over the waiting response, expecting to hear "K-108, I'm 10-4," the dispatcher began feeling a moment of dread. Upon receiving no response for over a minute and repeating the safety check a second time, the dispatcher asked a Chase County sheriff's deputy and another trooper miles away to patrol the area to locate Conroy.

Several minutes before the dispatcher began calling for Conroy, a passing motorist by the name of Steven Cahoon witnessed Conroy's patrol car sitting alongside the road. The red light on the roof was not flashing, nor were his rear "wig-wag" warning lights on. The patrol car did, however, have the four-way flashers going. Mr. Cahoon passed by the patrol car and saw Conroy lying in the ditch. Panicked, he pulled his pickup truck onto the shoulder ahead of the patrol car and got out. As Mr. Cahoon checked further, he confirmed his suspicion—the man in the ditch was wearing a Kansas Highway Patrol Trooper uniform—lying face down in the ditch away from the patrol car. As Steven Cohoon looked at Conroy's lifeless body, he knew the trooper was dead. Within minutes, other truck drivers and passing motorists began stopping to check out the scene.

Steven Cohoon, somewhat in shock and fully aware of the gravity of the matter, became a crime scene protector without actually knowing it. Cohoon had a background in security. He instantly jumped into action, keeping the people who had stopped from walking up to and around Conroy and trampling the crime scene.

As the call from Steven Cahoon came in via a citizen's band radio to the turnpike authority, the attendant telephoned the Kansas Highway Patrol Dispatch Center. Dispatch centers in Chase and Butler County received immediate notification and sent many officers to the location.

Shortly after they broadcast the call, a motorist provided the dispatcher with information describing the suspect vehicle. It is unknown if the passing motorist, who had seen the initial car stop occur, was monitoring a citizen's band radio or scanner; however, the motorist recalled seeing a large Cadillac-style car being stopped by Conroy's patrol car.

Within minutes, Butler County deputies, along with their command staff and Kansas State Troopers, swarmed the crime scene. Medical personnel from Butler County EMS Services arrived, and Paramedic/EMT Ray Long and Mitch Roberts checked Conroy's vital signs, finding none. Police had blocked off the area, cordoning it off for forensic investigators to take charge. They documented potential evidence with photographs, measurements and plaster casts. As they examined and processed the crime scene, someone ordered Conroy's body taken to Saint Francis Medical Center in Wichita. Ray Long and Mitch Roberts left the scene with Conroy in their ambulance at 9:59 am, arriving at Saint Francis at 11:00 am.

A wrecker removed Conroy's patrol car to Kansas Highway Patrol headquarters for a full detailed search. The authorities notified all state troopers and instructed them to search their assigned areas for the suspect vehicle.

Trooper Nate Sparks, working out of Junction City's regional office, was already on duty and began moving south on US Highway 77 from Junction City. Trooper Tony Van Buren, working out of Manhattan, began patrolling south and east toward the turnpike. Both would later play a pivotal role in what would soon transpire.

In the meantime, after committing this heinous act, Nelms, Myrick and Swain sped away northbound on the Kansas Turnpike. About four miles from the crime scene, Myrick threw Conroy's ticket book out the window where it landed in a grass field, near a bridge along the turnpike. Unsure of their location and lacking direction, they pulled into a gas station six miles from the murder scene.

Inside the store, Nelms purchased twelve dollars' worth of gasoline, a can of oil and a few snacks, as if going on a normal road trip. After gassing the Mercury, Nelms reversed course and began driving a short distance to the south, where he entered the US Route-77 northbound off-ramp. Nelms knew he had to go north.

Just south of the Dickinson County line, Nelms and his passengers were now northbound on US Route-77 headed towards Herington. While fleeing the area, Nelms determined the Mercury was not running well and wished to steal another car, if possible. Nelms began telling Myrick and Swain he wanted to steal another car, informing the men that he would probably have to kill someone at a farmhouse to do so. In less than ten minutes, the consequences of the right-hand turn would become apparent to all three of them.

8: THE SHOOTOUT

At 7:05 am, the phone rang as it hung on the east wall of the kitchen in a two-story home in Herington, Kansas. Having just finished shaving; Trooper Charlie Smith strolled from his bathroom to the ringing telephone.

"Hello," Smith answered.

"Trooper Smith?" the dispatcher asked.

"Yes, this is Trooper Smith," answered Smith.

Charlie listened as the dispatcher gave the information regarding the killing of Trooper O'Brien, happening just hours earlier. The only information the dispatcher could say for sure was that the suspected killer could be traveling in a light-colored, Cadillac-style vehicle, and they believed the suspect had stolen Trooper O'Brien's gun.

Charlie finished dressing in his freshly pressed Highway Patrol uniform, kissed his wife Edna goodbye, and headed toward his patrol car parked in his driveway, just as Conroy had done some eight hours earlier.

Charlie knew Conroy. Not well, but they had spoken on several occasions. Heartbreak and sadness filled him. A tall man, standing 6 feet 3 inches tall, an individual who was imposing as well as impressive. Charlie had made a name for himself around Dickinson County, Kansas, as a hard-working lawman. He was always professional, with a knack for sniffing out criminal activity and making high-profile arrests. He was no rookie. He was a seasoned cop who would take the killing of one of his brothers in blue personally.

Leaving his Herington home at 7:25 am, Charlie drove to the intersection of US 56 and US 77 highways and turned right. Before even having a sip of coffee to help wake himself up, Charlie, without delay, left town immediately to search for the individuals suspected of committing the murder. Eight miles—that's the distance that stood between Charlie and his goal; a relatively short distance before his search would be over and he would find what he was looking for.

At 7:33 am, while driving south on US 77, Charlie topped a slight hill south of Herington. As he crested the rise, he met a car, which instantly caused his cop's intuition to kick in. A large, light-colored, four-door Mercury Marquis sped past him. Everything about the car, catching his attention. Charlie clocked the Mercury's speed at 63 miles per hour in the 55 - mile - per-hour zone, the same speed Conroy had earlier stopped Myrick for. Charlie could see there were at least two men inside the car. The car's description precisely matched the one Kansas police were seeking.

A cop's intuition is like the feeling you get while fishing and you experience that big tug or jerk at the end of a fishing pole when the big fish bites. This feeling came over Trooper Charlie Smith just as the Mercury zipped past him, northbound. The driver immediately sped up and fled, reaching speeds over 100-mph. Charlie chased after them in his patrol cruiser, determined not to let this car get away until he confirmed whether these were the suspects everyone was searching for.

The chase continued northbound on US Highway 77 toward Herington. A Herington Police Department officer headed south towards the Mercury, and many troopers stationed further north in Junction City and Manhattan had already started heading south to join the chase. The chance of outrunning Charlie would be an exercise in futility. As Charlie notified dispatch of his chase, along with the vehicle's description, every cop in central Kansas went on high alert.

As Nelms fled northward, he knew he was facing a grim and desperate situation with few choices. He could have a shootout or try to escape in a high-speed chase. Four miles south of Herington, Nelms attempted to outrun Trooper Smith by taking a dirt road. The Mercury slowed to a manageable speed and suddenly turned east onto a dirt road, which turned out to be nothing more than a dirt path leading into a farmer's grazing field.

Hitting the dirt road, Nelms floored it, accelerating at high speeds towards his fight for freedom. At the end of the road, Nelms found a locked gate blocking the field entrance. Nelms smashed the Mercury through the gate and sped into an open grass pasture, which was closed off by a hedgerow near a creek along the east and a deep ditch to the north. He had simply driven into a field and was out of options to escape.

With Charlie hot on their tail, Nelms spun the Mercury around, throwing grass and dirt behind the car, making it clear he had nowhere to go but back to where he came from. Heading back toward the gate, the Mercury sped across the field. The engine roared as Nelms shoved it with all his might. As the dust cleared, the Mercury sped toward Trooper Smith, who saw the front seat passenger, Swain, jump from the car, falling to the ground before rolling and getting back to his feet and running to the east. Swain ran towards a tree row as the Mercury, with its two remaining passengers, continued speeding directly towards him.

As Trooper Charlie Smith continued calling the chase over the radio, everyone, including Charlie, suspected he was indeed chasing the people responsible for killing Trooper O'Brien. As the Mercury charged toward him, Charlie could see Nelms was on a kamikaze mission, heading straight toward his patrol car. With less than one hundred yards between them, Trooper Smith had only seconds to decide his next move. This could be, and probably would be, the most important decision he ever made in his law enforcement career. This quick decision could cost him his life.

He could either stop and block the entrance preventing an escape, or enter the field and continue straight toward the Mercury, which was speeding directly towards his patrol car. Trooper Smith stopped them in their tracks. As the Mercury continued speeding straight toward his patrol cruiser, Trooper Smith veered to his left and slammed into the Mercury head on, disabling it. The collision was teeth-rattling. It was as if Charlie had run straight into a brick wall. The crash was so loud, anyone within a quarter mile could have heard it. Metal folding up and glass breaking, followed by an intense sudden stop. Just as Charlie had braced for impact, bullets began flying from the Mercury, striking Charlie's windshield. Nelms, the driver, fired shots, sticking his pistol out of the open car window.

Charlie saw the red flames coming from Nelms pistol barrel after each shot, even in broad daylight. Charlie could also see the passenger in the back seat pointing a handgun out the passenger side of the car; however, the passenger was not firing at Trooper Smith. Observing the passenger pull the trigger, Trooper Smith concluded the firearm was likely malfunctioning or was being fired without ammunition.

Trooper Smith's windshield began shattering as each bullet slammed through it, with glass shards raining onto his uniform shirt and torso. Bullets fired by Nelms missed Trooper Smith, who leaned as far to his right as he could to duck his head below the dashboard. With both vehicles disabled, this had become a gunfight in a rural area. As Charlie ducked down, away from the bullets flying through his windshield, he grabbed his service revolver from his left-handed holster. Once armed, Trooper Smith sat upright and joined the gunfight by firing several shots through his own windshield toward Nelms, the driver of the Mercury.

Trooper Charlie Smith let loose a barrage of gunfire from his revolver, each round directed at Nelms, who was now hiding behind the Mercury's driver's door. When confronted with equal firepower, Nelms' response of fleeing did not surprise Trooper Smith. As Nelms and Charlie exchanged gunfire, the second suspect in the rear passenger seat, Myrick, fled on foot to get away from the gunfire. Myrick ran as fast as he could to the northeast toward Swain.

As Trooper Charlie Smith emptied his service revolver, he switched to his backup gun, a Smith and Wesson Model 20. Exiting his patrol car, he fired at Nelms, who spun and ran toward the Mercury's trunk to reload. Smith called over his radio for backup, "Shots fired, shots fired, send back-up."

Not having the luxury of time to reload the revolver, Trooper Smith exited his patrol car and moved along the driver's side toward his trunk, putting distance between him and Nelms. Shots from Nelms' handgun rang out, and Smith heard the bullets whizzing overhead and puncturing car metal. He used the patrol car as a shield until he could re-arm himself. Smith opened the trunk to retrieve his shotgun. After emptying his revolvers and making it to his trunk, Smith pulled his shotgun from its mount and chambered a round of double-aught buck (00 buck) into the weapon.

Seven rounds. This is what the shotgun held in the extended magazine tube. Charlie peered around the rear of his patrol car, leveling his shotgun, and brought Nelms into view over the front sight before unloading on him. Each trigger pull cycled the shotgun's action repeatedly, shell after shell. No one within fifty yards would have been safe. Two pellets struck Nelms in the face. One entered his left cheek beside his mouth, and one pellet entered Nelms' left eye. As Nelms felt the sting of the buckshot impact, he jumped away from the Mercury, running eastward away from the crash site. One last blast from Trooper Smith's shotgun would add two more pellets to Nelms back and shoulder as he fled. The Mercury's windshield, top, hood and driver's door took most of the mutilation from the buckshot pellets. However, Trooper Smith caused enough injury to Nelms to stop the shootout and assist in the suspect's capture.

Nelms, armed with a Colt Lawman .357 revolver, began running across the grass field toward the other suspects, who had fled to the east. Nelms had fired the revolver empty and, after reloading it with six fresh rounds, had fired five of the six at Trooper Smith before fleeing. Trooper Smith returned to his driver's seat and radioed dispatch, notifying them of the suspects fleeing in a northeasterly direction. Trooper Smith had survived this harrowing shootout. He was bound and determined to catch the suspects before they had any opportunity to kill again.

9: THE SEARCH FOR A KILLER

Herrington, road to where the shootout took place. Courtesy of the Smoky Hill Museum; Salina Newspaper Archival Collection.

Herington police officers, along with Deputies Tom Furman (Marion County) and Dick Malik (Morris County), arrived at Trooper Smith's damaged patrol car within ten minutes.

Chief Harold Furman of the Council Grove Police Department arrived soon afterward, accompanied by Officers John Quinn, Benny Furman, and Charles Robidoux. Law enforcement formed a quick-response task force. They began heading out to cover the residences to the north and east, which were within walking distance of where the shootout had occurred.

Within two hours, over two hundred Kansas law enforcement officers were on the scene to ensure the suspect's capture. Several of the local farmers overheard Trooper Smith's calls for help as the radio traffic crossed their scanner frequencies. The farmers decided it would be best to arm themselves with deer rifles and shotguns and head out to canvas the area. One farmer, a wealthy rancher with a helicopter, added his arsenal to the hunt and was soon airborne in search of the suspects.

Helicopter arrives to canvas the area. Courtesy of the Smoky Hill Museum; Salina Newspaper Archival Collection.

Trooper Smith was concerned about the two farms located north and east because there could be occupants inside, unaware and off guard from what had transpired. So, the deputies drove to the farm, actively warning the residents. They began searching the outer farm buildings to ensure the criminals were not hiding within. Eventually, police from all over central Kansas showed up to assist with this slow and dangerous job.

Law enforcement help arrived from as far as Salina, McPherson County, and even Topeka

(KBI agents). Within one hour of the search beginning, Nelms, injured and bleeding, as well as Myrick were located as they hid under brush along a creek bank nearly one-half mile from the shootout scene. Nelms had thrown the Colt Lawman revolver into a small pond and hid his FIE-branded .38 Special Derringer near his hiding spot along the creek. Myrick also concealed his RG-40 .38 Special revolver along the creek bank. When Nelms emerged from the brush, blood was streaming down his left cheek. Crawling from his hiding place, he came face-to-face with troopers ready to shoot.

As troopers arrested Nelms and Myrick, both were unarmed as they had discarded their weapons as they ran. Trooper Carl McDonald slowly walked the path between the suspects' car and their hiding place and spotted the RG-40 revolver, which had been dry fired by Myrick during the shootout, lying on the ground near a tree line.

The small, chrome two-shot Derringer found by Trooper Jerry Downie was the same Derringer pointed at Chad Simmons during the jewelry robbery in Springfield, Missouri. Simmons would later testify and identify the gun as being the same Derringer used by Nelms in the jewelry store robbery.

After their arrests, officers walked the suspects to waiting cruisers to interview them. Nelms, being defiant and saying absolutely nothing to law enforcement, demanded medical attention.

Authorities took Nelms to the hospital in Herington, where medical staff cleaned and examined him. Doctors then ordered his transfer to St. John's Hospital in Salina and later to a trauma center in Wichita. His injuries were beyond what the hospitals in Herington or Salina could treat. Myrick, being advised of his Miranda rights by

Above Trooper Charlie Smith's patrol car with troopers and other law enforcement and local farmers canvasing the area and below the suspects Mercury Marquis. Left a local farmer helps canvas the area. Courtesy of the Smoky Hill Museum; Salina Newspaper Archival Collection.

Salina Chief of Police, John Woody, was not overly forthcoming with information. The only information he provided was, "I did not kill that Trooper."

    Troopers Nate Sparks, Tony VanBuren, Jerry Downie and Mick Allen continued scouring the area looking for the third suspect. As they did, they noticed something odd. It was nearly two hours into the manhunt when they walked near a bridge along a ditch and found the last suspect. Trooper Downie noticed something was off about the dirt around a pile of brush. As he stood staring at the pile of brush, his mind must have felt like an electrical jolt went through it. Trooper Downie silently motioned Troopers Sparks, VanBuren and Allen to rush to his aid. As he stood on the creek bank, looking downward into a pile of brush, Downie spotted the bottom of a bare foot sticking slightly out from the brush. "I could see his toes," Trooper Downie would later tell his fellow partners.

    As Trooper Nate Sparks commanded the hiding suspect to give up and show himself, Trooper VanBuren approached the ditch toward the suspect, pointing his handgun at the pile. Trooper Sparks yelled orders to the hiding suspect. As the sounds of many approaching officers echoed through the woods, the suspect, Swain, crawled out from under the heavy brush and surrendered. As Swain gave himself up, Trooper Mick Allen handcuffed Swain, bringing the manhunt to an end.

Left and above, farm area where suspects surrender and are arrested. Courtesy of the Smoky Hill Museum; Salina Newspaper Archival Collection.

The third suspect, Swain, was clearly scared and shaking from what he had endured. Swain was a twenty-one-year-old man from Jackson, Georgia. Swain was wearing only dark-colored pants. He had gotten rid of his shirt, shoes and socks and was unarmed; however, he would soon show the officers what they needed to connect the dots to Trooper Conroy O'Brien's killing.

Upon discovery, Swain's Miranda rights were read to him by Trooper Nate Sparks as they stood in a field, surrounded by several farmers. Somewhat in shock and with no good options in sight, he divulged everything he knew about the Matfield Green killing. Swain held a degree of guilt; although he did not fire the shot, Swain knew he should have tried something to stop Nelms from killing the trooper and putting all of them in this unbelievable mess they were now in.

For Swain, what had started as a trip to Denver to see his family members had gone completely off the rails. The events that transpired noticeably scared and shook Swain. He made it clear to

Above, Salina Police Department Chief, John Woody interviews suspect, Walter Myrick in the patrol car. Courtesy of the Smoky Hill Museum; Salina Newspaper Archival Collection.

law enforcement officers he was not the person responsible for killing Trooper Conroy O'Brien. Inside the police car, Swain was cooperative, sharing everything needed to move the investigation forward.

During Swain's interview, he divulged information about the location of Conroy's ticket book and handgun, which only someone involved would have known. This single authentic piece of evidence would definitively determine the fate of all three suspects. Swain told the police Myrick had thrown the items out of the car during the chase and was willing to show them where they could find the items. As Swain began baring his soul to save his own skin, Myrick began doing the same, but in smaller bits and with details left out. Myrick was also blaming the killing entirely on Nelms, stating Nelms had acted alone and he had nothing to do with it, other than being a witness.

Geary County Sheriff Jim Gross and Kansas Highway Patrol Sgt. Ted Thompson soon located the Smith and Wesson Model 19, a .357 revolver stolen from Conroy and then used to kill him. They

> "It's a black day gentleman."
> —said an unnamed Kansas Highway Patrol Trooper, reported by the *Parsons Sun*, May 25, 1978

Above, law enforcement process what has happened. Courtesy of the Smoky Hill Museum; Salina Newspaper Archival Collection.

found the gun 112 feet south of the Dickinson County line and 29 feet east of the east roadside of US Highway 77, in Marion County. The gun had two empty cartridges and four loaded rounds in the cylinder.

Swain told the police Myrick had thrown the stolen revolver out of the rear window of the Mercury as soon as Trooper Smith began turning around to pursue them.

Back at Milepost 94 at Matfield Green, a group of over twenty officers finally found the stolen ticket book after conducting a thorough grid search of the area Swain had described. They found the ticket book lying in a grass field off the northbound turnpike lanes, approximately four miles north of the murder scene. The last ticket listed the name Tommy McClendon, but Myrick's birthdate appeared on the same line. The ticket was incomplete, and neither Trooper O'Brien nor Myrick had signed it, because in the struggle Trooper O'Brien's flashlight and pen had fallen to the floorboard of his patrol car.

As an ambulance transported Nelms from Salina to Wesley Medical Center in Wichita due to his extensive injuries, law officers took Myrick and Swain to the Butler County jail and booked them for murder.

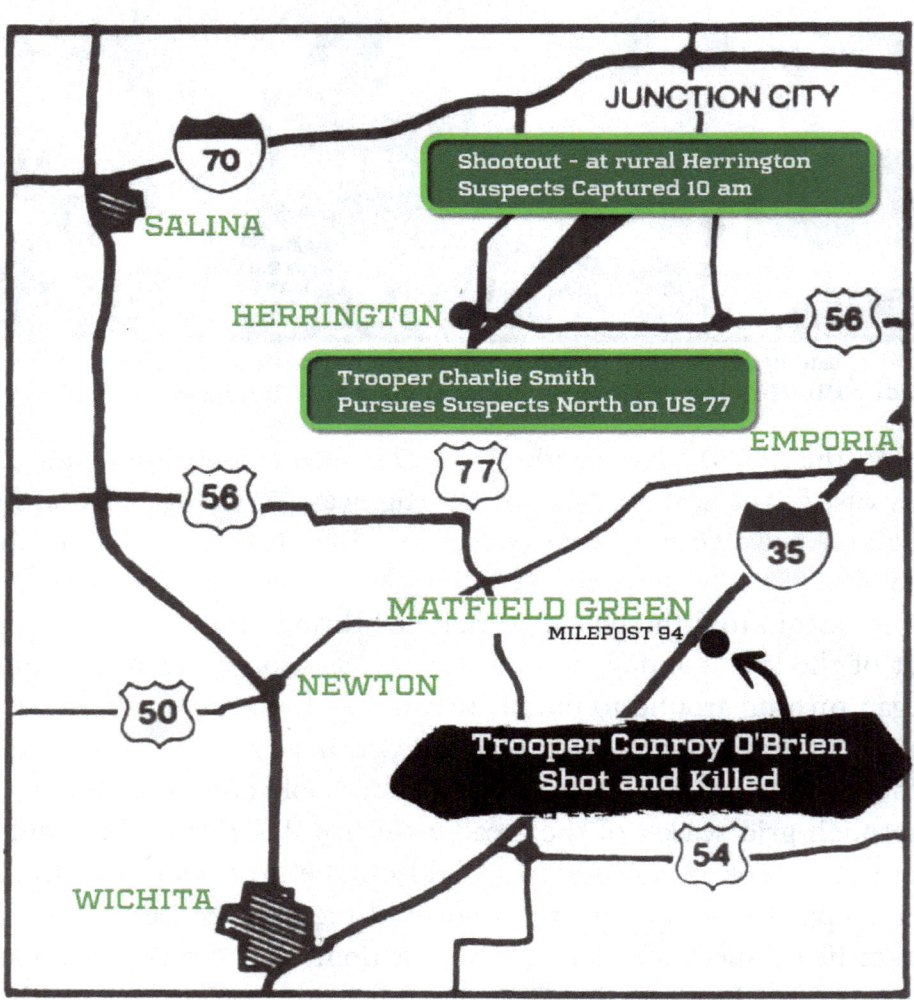

10: THE AUTOPSY & Dr. NOGUCHI

A around 10:00 am, Dr. Thomas Noguchi was finishing up his presentation, informing some of the nation's leading pathologists about the latest and greatest medical breakthroughs in the field of forensic science, when the telephone rang at the Broadview Hotel in downtown Wichita. Doctor William Eckert, the Sedgwick County Coroner, who was hosting the international forensic conference, was being summoned to the telephone. Dr. Eckert, along with the Sedgwick County Medical Examiner's Office, was hosting the conference every other year and had arranged the conference gathering to be at the Broadview Hotel. At the 1978 International Association of Forensic Science conference, the keynote speaker was none other than the world-renowned "coroner to the stars." Dr. Thomas Noguchi from the Los Angeles Medical Examiner's Office. Dr. Noguchi and Dr. Eckert were not only colleagues in forensic pathology but also good friends.

People in the medical field knew Noguchi as the "Coroner to the Stars" because he had performed autopsies on movie stars, such as Marilyn Monroe, John Belushi, William Holden, Janis Joplin, Sharon Tate and Natalie Wood. He also performed the autopsy on Senator Robert F. Kennedy after his assassination in June 1968. Dr. Noguchi was world-renowned as a true specialist in his field. Drs. Noguchi and Eckert, among others, were transforming the coroner profession into an investigative one. These professionals had teams of doctors, specialists and criminal investigators assigned to their offices, and a major shift in the manner of their work was taking place in 1978. As a result, primarily because of Dr. Noguchi, forensic science was undergoing significant changes and advancements. This conference represented significant progress for the profession.

Dr. Noguchi began his work in the office of the Chief Medical Examiner-Coroner for the County of Los Angeles in 1961. His early career gained public attention after the Marilyn Monroe autopsy. After authoring the autopsy report for Senator Robert F. Kennedy, Dr. Noguchi would be called a conspiracy theorist, as he reported Kennedy was actually shot from behind, four times, which would prove counter to any evidence that showed Sirhan Sirhan could have been the shooter.

As Dr. Eckert picked up the telephone at the Broadview Hotel's front desk, he was immediately briefed about the murder of a Kansas Highway Patrol trooper. The KBI asked him to perform an autopsy in a timely manner. Dr. Eckert told the caller from the KBI he would handle the matter as soon as the body arrived at Saint Francis Hospital. He also told the caller he would bring Dr. Thomas Noguchi along to assist in the matter.

At 11:00 am, Trooper Conroy O'Brien's body arrived at Saint Francis Hospital in Wichita. They wheeled him into the hospital morgue, followed by Captain Dean Jost of the Butler County Sheriff's Office, Trooper M.G. Kelly, KBI Agent Steve Couch, and Doctors William Eckert, James Sweeney and Thomas Noguchi.

Dr. Thomas Noguchi forensic scientist. Courtesy of the Smoky Hill Museum; Salina Newspaper Archival Collection, File Photo c1985.

Dr. Eckert performed the autopsy, while Dr. Noguchi assisted and supervised the autopsy. It was not a competition between the doctors. They were all on the same team.

During the medical examination, officials removed all personal effects from Conroy's uniform. Dr. Eckert located a small pistol tucked into the shoulder holster under Conroy's left armpit. The medical examiner also located Conroy's small pocket-sized blood-soaked New Testament inside his right uniform shirt pocket. It was as much a part of his uniform as his badge and gun had been.

No one knows why Dr. Noguchi assisted; however, many suspect that after Dr. Eckert informed him of the killing, Dr. Noguchi joined on his own. It is unlikely Dr. Eckert would have turned down Dr. Noguchi's forensic expertise and help.

During the initial examination of the body, Dr. Eckert found an injury to Conroy's scalp where a revolver struck him as he faced away from the suspect. It was determined this had happened before the murder. Dr. Eckert determined that two bullets struck Conroy's left skull. The death was determined to be instantaneous when the first bullet hit the left ear. The death was determined to have occurred as Conroy was lying on his stomach, with his head turned slightly to his left. Both bullets had traveled through Conroy's skull and exited into the earth below him. The investigation revealed gunshot residue and slight stippling burns on both Conroy's forearms, indicating he positioned his hands beside his head when shot. It was also determined the shooter had been within one foot of Conroy O'Brien.

Conroy' pocket sized blood-soaked New Testament. Image courtesy of Tanda O'Brien.

In Los Angeles, Dr. Noguchi had used body molds to help prosecutors show jurors exactly how the death of a victim occurred. These molds illustrated the stabbing or gunshot wounds, and the trajectory the impact came from. This was a relatively new technique. Dr. Noguchi instructed Dr. Eckert on making the "injury mold" to be used by the prosecutors in the courtroom. The team completed the mold of Conroy's head injuries and autopsy at 4:00 pm. Using the molds, prosecutors could show the killing at point-blank range. At the conclusion of the autopsy, the authorities released Conroy O'Brien's remains to the Elliott Mortuary funeral home in Hutchinson.

The model and type of weapons involved in this investigation were similar to the following public domain stock images.

Colt Lawman   FIE .38

Smith & Wesson 19   Derringer

11: A WIFE'S GRIEF

At approximately 7:30 am, Tanda O'Brien, five months pregnant, lay asleep in her bed, her breath slow and even, rising and falling gently in the quiet room. A sudden, frantic banging on her front door jolted her awake, her heart leaping into her throat. Sleepily, Tanda shuffled towards her front door, the chilling premonition of Conroy's fate a heavy weight on her heart. She would later state she just knew in her bones Conroy was dead.

As Tanda opened the door without waiting for an invitation, Trooper Alan Bachelor, Conroy's training officer, friend and neighbor, rushed inside, embracing Tanda. Shaken, he informed Tanda someone had killed Conroy. Alan Bachelor, filled with his own grief, stood in shock as he told her that her husband was not coming home. Conroy was dead, the victim of a shooting. As a dark veil of immense grief engulfed her, Tanda broke down and began weeping uncontrollably. Trooper Bachelor stayed with Tanda for most of the morning and would later help in making the notifications to family members.

During the initial hours after Trooper Bachelor had notified Tanda of the murder, she called Trooper Howard Fehrenbacher. He was a man known all around her hometown of Kinsley. With tears flowing and deep sobbing, Tanda asked Howard if he would give the death notification to her father and mother. She could not muster the energy to call her father. A short time later, after absorbing the shock, Tanda called her mother-in-law to relay this devastating news.

So many people who loved and respected Conroy O'Brien had felt the weight of the tragedy. This deep pain traveled throughout the O'Brien circle of family and friends like an unreal black cloud, and no one really knew how to confront or deal with it. To each of them, the news was so shocking, so utterly beyond belief, that it left them speechless.

The shattering of the O'Brien and Parnell families, the small town of Abbyville, and the Kansas Highway Patrol—a fraternity bound by duty and now grief—from this murder would echo for years to come, leaving a trail of broken hearts. Many felt robbed of precious life moments that would never come to fruition. Conroy's funeral would actually stand at the forefront of the feeling of being cheated for so many, and for so many years to follow.

This was not an expected funeral because of old age. No, this pain hurt on a much deeper level. The black veil that had dropped onto Tanda fell over everyone who attended the funeral service in this small community. The family held Conroy O'Brien's funeral inside Abbyville Elementary School's gymnasium, where Conroy had played many times in his youth. This was the best place for the community to gather and grieve. Over 300 gathered to honor and mourn a man they respected so deeply.

Conroy O'Brien, a vibrant twenty-six-year-old brimming with life and love, died cruelly—ripped from his family, never to hold his precious baby daughter, whose arrival he had eagerly awaited. In his absence, silence roared. Injustice pressed heavily on his widow's chest. The scale of his murder defied comprehension; no one could fathom how or why it had happened. Bitterness blanketed the community, each person painfully aware of the wrong done, struggling to make sense of the fate that had robbed them. Grief hung thick in the air, unspoken yet deeply felt.

Many sent beautiful flower arrangements perched on stands around the casket, which held a man lost entirely too soon. One could feel the sadness dripping off of each of them.

Conroy laid in the open casket, dressed in his Highway Patrol uniform after being prepared by his dear friend, Doyle Eiling. Doyle had known Conroy as a young child and had grown up with him, attending school from kindergarten through their high school years. Conroy's childhood friend had the immense duty of preparing Conroy for his funeral. Eiling, an employee of the Elliott Mortuary Company in Hutchinson, Kansas, had to do the unimaginable—after the medical examiner released the body, he prepared his friend's remains. Although possibly the hardest emotional endeavor he would have to endure, he prepared the remains for the open casket viewing and funeral. Tanda, thinking back on this day as she walked to her husband's casket, remembers looking down at Conroy and feeling the need to touch up the makeup, making sure Conroy was perfect for his final day in front of his loved ones and friends.

Tanda O'Brien being hugged by Trooper Chuck Wickham, along with her father, Otis Parnell (above).

At the cemetery, friends and family found it unbelievably muddy as it had rained hard the night before. Before the graveside services could even begin, several troopers had to help push the hearse out of a mudhole. Solid earth was scarce as everything seemed slimed in a heavy mud. Parking and unloading the hearse was no simple task. Several troopers had muddy boots as they stood at attention for their brother in blue.

The pallbearers were Allen Bachelor, Jim Mosher, Steve Jensen, Ed Vohs, Floyd Keiffer and Ed Bartowski. Each a friend. Each a fellow State trooper. Together, they rolled the casket from the back door of the hearse and carried Conroy to the pedestal. As they lowered Conroy's casket into the earth, Tanda and her father simply melted with pure grief.

Toward the tail end of Conroy's funeral service, an Oklahoma Highway Patrol Honor Guard unit, which had traveled to Abbyville to pay their respects for a fallen brother, received a notification of another tragedy. Four Oklahoma troopers had just died in a shootout near Oklahoma City, and the honor guard members had to leave the burial to rush home and help deal with their own emergency, occurring in Oklahoma.

Three weeks after the funeral, when the shock of his murder began setting in and people began realizing the gravity of the entire situation. Kansas Governor Robert F. Bennett, upon learning of the situation, presented Trooper Charlie Smith with the governor's award in recognition of his heroic capture of the suspects. On Monday, June 14, 1978, Trooper Smith along with his wife and children traveled to the Topeka State Capitol where Governor Bennett presented him with "The Governor's Award." It happened at a small and mostly unseen ceremony in the Governor's office.

Kansas Governor Robert F. Bennett hands Trooper Charlie Smith (pictured left) an award as his family proudly watches. Courtesy of The Herington Times.

Fifty years after the murder of her husband, Tanda would admit that the veil of darkness which came upon her on May 24, 1978, has never really left. A ghost of pain, a shadow of suffering, lingers on her pretty face, a testament to the torment that still holds her captive.

Tanda reflected. "I was cheated out of a wonderful husband."

12: LET'S MAKE A DEAL

After the arrests of Jimmie K. Nelms, Walter Myrick and Stanford Swain, a case for criminal prosecution needed preparation. The task of building this case fell to Norman Manley, Deputy County Attorney for Butler County, Kansas. Following the murder and arrests, he conferred with numerous law enforcement officials to collect evidence for the prosecution.

As Manley sat at his desk at the Butler County Attorney's office, he took notes, which he soon made into a typed document. When he was done, he had created a two-page masterpiece known as "Information." Attorneys across the country create this document daily. It serves one purpose: to inform a court of facts, showing a specific person had committed the elements of specific crimes. The information is a charging document, similar to an affidavit, which he would submit to the district court.

Once attorney Manley issued the information to the Butler County District Court, the ball would soon begin rolling. The County Attorney usually receives an affidavit from law enforcement to prepare their information document, but in this instance, Manley used officers' information to create the document on his own, without a formal affidavit.

After someone files the information, the court clerk will publish the document by stamp filing it in their office, certifying the document as official, and submitting it to the court for charges. A judge then reviews the information and issues a warrant, charging a specific person with a crime.

Norman Manley meticulously listed out the facts and criminal charges being brought against the three defendants. Count number one from a portion of the information filed against Nelms stated he did "unlawfully, willfully, maliciously, deliberately and with premeditation, kill and murder a certain human being, to wit: Conroy O'Brien by shooting the same with a certain gun pursuant to K.S.A. 21-3401."

The document added charges against Nelms for aggravated assault, kidnapping, aggravated robbery and conspiracy. Attorney Manley drafted the same charges in separate information/complaint documents against Myrick and Swain. The county clerk's office certified the information documents and forwarded them to Judge

John Jaworsky for his signature on arrest warrants against the three suspected murderers.

Following the charges against the three suspects, Judge Jaworsky was responsible for protecting the defendants' rights. To ensure this, his first order was to appoint counsel to each of the defendants.

Judge Jaworsky arraigned and assigned legal counsel to each of the suspects by appointing the following attorneys:

- Wallace F. Davis to represent Jimmie K. Nelms.
- Doyle Eugene White Jr. to represent Walter Myrick.
- David All to represent Stanford Swain.

Upon meeting David All, Swain immediately expressed his desire to cooperate with law enforcement and confess everything. After Swain explained the entire crime spree to his attorney, David All believed allowing Swain to "tell all" would in fact be in Swain's best interest, and he believed he could obtain a conviction and prison sentence for reduced charge(s) for Swain. Attorney All called Norman Manley, arranging for a meeting with the County Attorney.

Once the arraignments concluded, District Judge Page W. Benson took over the case in his courtroom, managing the trial from the initial motion to the trial's closing statement.

While renowned in Kansas legal circles, Judge Benson lacked experience with murder trials of this scale and importance. Judge Benson knew also that higher courts would meticulously scrutinize all his future decisions. Judge Benson's primary concern was not a legal matter, but rather the security of his courtroom, both inside and out. It remains unknown why Judge Benson was so overly concerned about security, or if someone had informed him of specific threats to the proceedings. Due to his concerns, he applied the following rules to the pre-trial hearings:

1. "Armed officers will be posted at exit/entry doors leading inside of the courthouse."

2. "Armed officers will be posted outside and within the courtroom entrance."

3. "A metal detector will be utilized prior to any person entering the courtroom."

To assist in keeping all hearings calm and orderly, he added specific decorum rules to go along with the security measures.

1. "All persons desiring access to the courtroom are subject to inspection by metal detectors. Packages and other closed items will not be permitted in the courtroom."

2. "Members of the public attending court proceedings shall be in their place before court convenes. Late arrivals will not be seated until the next recess."

3. "Persons leaving in the middle of proceedings will not be re-admitted until the next recess. Lingering in the halls near the courtroom will not be permitted."

Judge Benson made it known that only law enforcement would have guns on the property and no one was going to act out or otherwise disrupt the proceedings, no matter how they felt about the defendants or the court.

These strict security measures and decorum rules were not something commonly ordered by Judge Benson or any other judge in Butler County. Judge Benson's intuition and foresight regarding the court proceedings prompted him to order courtroom rules for everyone's safety.

Judge Benson then gave all attorneys orders to have motions filed by specific dates so the trial would not get bogged down in last-minute theatrics. Judge Benson ran what he considered a tight ship. He wanted no surprises from either the defense or the state.

The court clerks scheduled a preliminary hearing for mid-

June 1978. However, before a hearing could occur, attorneys David All and Norman Manley notified the court that Swain would change his plea to guilty in exchange for lesser charges. Manley informed Judge Benson that Swain would plead guilty to a charge of aiding a felon and illegal possession of a firearm. Swain had agreed to testify against both Nelms and Myrick. He would also accept a prison sentence of between six and twenty years.

This development infuriated attorneys White Jr. and Davis, as it basically destroyed their antagonistic defense argument. Nelms and Myrick waived their preliminary hearings and moved forward with their court cases.

One of the first motions (following the Swain announcement) was a joint request by attorneys White Jr. and Davis. They requested to have the trial severed into separate trials in order to provide fairness to each defendant. Judge Benson allowed the attorneys to argue their points, followed by his ruling. Judge Benson denied the motion on the grounds that all three defendants were present at the murder scene, and further, they had all taken part in the crime, and each was present at the shootout with Trooper Charlie Smith. Because of these facts, Judge Benson ruled there were no grounds to separate the cases.

Attorney Davis, representing Nelms, filed a motion for a change of venue, arguing that extensive negative media coverage created unacceptable prejudice, preventing a fair trial. As in many murder cases, news outlets/agencies report the details to the public within a region, and often statewide. The murder of a state trooper had most definitely been a statewide broadcast. Television news programs and newspapers across Kansas had relayed the story of the murder of Trooper Conroy O'Brien for the following weeks. This was something news outlets would widely report.

The Wichita Eagle, Council Grove Republic, Salina Journal and many other newspapers had front-page stories covering the crime. *The Wichita Eagle* printed photographs of officers walking the suspects out of the wooded area where they had found them hiding after the shootout south of Herington. Pictures depicted armed officers holding onto the suspect's arms during the arrest. Attorney Davis used these news stories, claiming the massive attention would sway the jury's opinion of the defendants, clearly, leading to an unfair trial.

During a hearing about the change of venue, attorney Davis brought forth witnesses from media outlets who testified about how this murder had been such a massive news story for days and weeks following the crime. Although Judge Benson listened to the testimony, it did not sway him. He ruled the publicity did not rise to the level that could interfere with a fair trial. Judge Benson denied the motion.

Several weeks before the start date, attorney All, along with his client, Swain, appeared before Judge Benson, where Swain pled guilty to the two lesser charges. Swain had a full debriefing with KBI investigators, explaining the events leading to Trooper Conroy O'Brien's death, before entering his plea.

KBI agents Gary Davis and Ray Macy, along with attorney David All, conducted the interview. Swain stated under oath he witnessed Nelms retrieve a handgun from the Mercury's glove-box, and heard Nelms make the statement, "I'm going to kill that cop," directly to Swain as they sat inside the Mercury. He further testified that Nelms snuck out of the Mercury and pointed the handgun at Trooper O'Brien, taking him hostage. Swain told the KBI investigators he witnessed Nelms and Myrick force Trooper O'Brien to walk away from the patrol car, at gunpoint, and down into the ditch behind the patrol car. Swain swore under oath that Myrick stood beside Nelms as Nelms first struck Trooper O'Brien in the head with the trooper's gun, knocking Conroy to the ground.

Swain said he sat inside the Mercury and watched Nelms shoot Trooper O'Brien in the head twice and Myrick and Nelms then ran back to the Mercury and told him (Swain) to grab a towel and wipe the cop's car down where Nelms had touched it. According to Swain, he grabbed a towel from the Mercury's back seat and then went to the patrol car. As he did, he wiped several areas of the trooper's car with the towel. Swain claimed he was terrified about the killing and, after doing what Nelms had ordered him to do, he returned to the Mercury. All three fled from the scene as soon as

Swain had gotten back to the Mercury.

For taking responsibility for his actions, completing the interview and testifying at the trial against Myrick and Nelms to assist the state, he could then have lesser charges and receive a reduced prison sentence of six to ten years. This plea deal did not sit well with either Nelms, Myrick or their attorneys.

The Swain plea deal also triggered another motion by the remaining defendants. The motion was a second request for a change of venue, after Nelms' attorney raised issues the Wichita Eagle and subsequent other newspapers printed: "The state has validated the testimony of their star witness...." The article further stated that prosecutor Manley stated: "Based on the evidence that we have, Swain pled guilty to what we believe he is guilty of." Norman Manley told the reporter that Swain had not seen one defendant for over two years and knew the other only slightly. Manley added, "I don't think he [Swain] had anything to do with it."

Nelms and Myrick felt their court case was hopeless from the start, due to Swain's publicized guilty plea and testimony. Again, for the second time, Nelms and Myrick had requested a change of venue because of the publication and Swain's documented plea deal. And yet again, Judge Benson denied their request, stating he "did not believe the news article could or would poison any juror's opinion."

Attorney Davis then filed a motion in limine—a pretrial motion to exclude evidence. The aim is to prevent the jury from being exposed to prejudicial, irrelevant, or inadmissible information. Davis assumed, and rightfully so, the state would introduce the evidence from the shootout in Dickinson County with Trooper Charlie Smith. Using this evidence might bolster the case against Nelms. Davis asked the court to prohibit any reference at trial regarding the shootout and not admit any evidence found from the shootout investigation, as he felt it was both overly damning, prejudicial to his client and had nothing at all to do with crimes occurring near Matfield Green. County Attorney Manley argued the shootout was absolutely a continuation of the murder of Trooper Conroy O'Brien as the defendants had possessed the same handguns in both Butler and Dickinson Counties. Both Nelms and Myrick had either shot at or pointed a gun and pulled the trigger during the shootout crime scene at another State Trooper. Manley clarified, in his mind, all the shootout evidence south of Herington could be directly linked to the murder of Trooper O'Brien.

Judge Benson agreed with the state and ordered the court to allow all evidence during the trial. The court clerks scheduled the trial for the two remaining defendants for August 21, 1978.

13: THE TRIAL

The remaining defendants waived the preliminary hearing, and the court granted no continuances. The criminal trial of Nelms and Myrick began on August 21, 1978.

Nelms' attorney Davis objected to the heavily guarded areas around the courtroom, and Myrick's attorney White Jr. agreed with this argument. Both defense attorneys Davis and White Jr. argued, "the security put off such a show of force that no citizen could see it as anything other than a lynch mob waiting to strike."

Judge Benson would hear none of it. "I am doing my due diligence in protecting all people within the building," he calmly stated to the attorneys. He quickly denied the argument. Judge Benson addressed the issue of court security as the court bailiff led the jurors into the courtroom:

> *Ladies and Gentlemen, certain efforts have been made and you have undoubtedly seen a large number of officers, but I don't want you to be concerned about the number of law enforcement officers around the courtroom at this time...The case involves Conroy O'Brien who was a member of the Kansas Highway Patrol and many officers, I am sure made the investigation and the mere fact that there are officers around here...shouldn't concern you.*

As the jury listened to Judge Benson, he explained he was certain most, if not all, the jurors had been subject to hearsay, or had read facts and/or opinions printed in the newspapers regarding the case. He explained the defendants were innocent until proven guilty and they must be tried nowhere except in this court of law.

After the second day of jury selection—known as *voir dire* (French for "to speak the truth")—some of these individuals became the selected jurors, fulfilling their duty as citizens in the judicial process. A total of twelve jurors—seven women and five men—along with two alternates, embarked on a case unlike anything they ever imagined being part of.

Conflicts between the defendants began almost immediately during the opening arguments and continued throughout the trial. The friends had become enemies, and this included the defense attorneys.

During the first witness testimony, attorney Davis started referring to Myrick by his nickname "Ironhead," as he had been called by his associates on the street. Attorney Davis had apparently done so to demean or belittle Myrick and make him look like a thug. Myrick's attorney, White Jr. adopted the same approach in retaliation. White Jr. began referring to Nelms by his nicknames of "Blanche" and "Black Jesus." During the trial, Nelms testified in his own defense. Testifying, Nelms accused Swain and Myrick of plotting to blame him during their police interview with Chief Woody in the back of a patrol car. Nelms testified he had been asleep in the back seat of the Mercury and woke up after hearing the gunshots, only to find Swain and Myrick standing over the slain trooper. However, the shoe impressions in the dirt matched the shoes Nelms wore.

Some of the testimony while Nelms was on the stand blaming Myrick for the crime got so heated that attorney White Jr. and Davis shouted at each other with such vicious outpouring the judge had to stop the proceedings and calm people down. Attorney Davis openly expressed his feelings about both Attorney White Jr. and All—claiming they were incompetent in blaming his client for this crime. His frustration had boiled over, and he let it show to the jury. Swain's plea deal, and the ruling not to sever the cases, obviously caused this anger. Myrick did not testify, making his defense primarily dependent upon the testimony and cross-examination of Swain in hopes the jury would fully believe Swain's version of the events. This legal strategy's flaw is that the jury did precisely what it aimed to prevent. Swain testified Nelms had pointed the trooper's gun at O'Brien as he lay in the ditch and he saw the flames from the gun being shot twice, and he testified Myrick had been right beside Nelms when the crime occurred and had not tried to stop Nelms or intervene. Swain also testified that after the killing and before the chase and shootout, Nelms told Swain, "if you tell anyone about what happened, I will kill your family."

During closing arguments, attorney Davis called Swain a "Hertz-rent-a-witness" out of sheer frustration. He also pointed out a few inconsistencies in his testimony compared to what the investigators claimed Swain had said during the initial interviews.

When it was Prosecutor Norman Manley's turn to close out the trial, he ended his closing statement with a masterful verbal display. Norman eloquently stated:

> *Sixty feet. That is how far they walked Trooper O'Brien. Sixty feet of premeditation and two bullets, not one...Because of Walter Myrick, Conroy O'Brien is in his grave just as surely as if Myrick had pulled the trigger himself. Last May 24, a young highway patrol trooper asked these two men, 'please don't do this to me.' Today, you hear these two defendants say 'Don't do this to me.' These men are guilty.*

The jury did not believe the testimony of Nelms, who had blamed the murder on both Swain and Myrick.

On August 30, 1978, the jury returned verdicts of guilty against both Nelms and Myrick for First Degree Murder, Kidnapping and Weapons violations. Nelms and Myrick's prior felony convictions led to the weapons charge. After the trial, Judge Benson scheduled a sentencing date for Nelms and Myrick.

Myrick's presence beside Nelms during the murder of Conroy O'Brien, without any attempt to intervene, made him equally culpable. Myrick prevented neither Conroy's kidnapping nor stopped Nelms from killing. Under the laws of Kansas, Myrick was just as culpable as Nelms himself.

Myrick felt this verdict was unfair, and in disbelief that everything turned against him, as if he had pulled the trigger. Myrick was in shock when the verdict against him had been read. He stood at the defense table with his head hung downward as if in a trance. However, he would soon wake up and begin his fight for freedom using the Kansas appeals process.

Dickinson County District Court never charged Nelms and Myrick for their involvement in the shootout with Trooper Charlie Smith. The Dickinson County Attorney's failure to file attempted murder and weapons violation charges remains unexplained. It's plausible the County Attorney may have felt the murder conviction in Butler County would be sufficient.

Motions for appeal followed. In this case, two appeals. And, for all the people who expected boring legal claims and lackluster legal banter, the level of interesting and somewhat entertaining information would soon shock them as it came from the appeals process. This case would prove to be anything but mundane.

The public rarely sees or cares to indulge in something as boring as an appeal brief or the findings from the court. However, when looking into a crystal ball of the Kansas Supreme Court case in Nelms and Myrick vs. The State of Kansas, one can only sit back, smile and enjoy the banter that ensued between their attorneys. Even a carefree civilian would be amused if they followed the appeals roadmap being laid out for the justices.

14: THE APPEAL

A s with all serious court convictions, most will undergo an appeals process. Many arguments made before or during trial, regardless of merit, may prompt an appeal. With this case being the murder of a state trooper, the trial judge knew every decision he/she made could be grounds for an appeal. As expected, Judge Benson's rulings each faced a challenge. Some challenges may have even sounded somewhat valid on paper; however, some were simply a last grasp toward hope.

In 1977, the State of Kansas created what is known today as the Kansas Court of Appeals. However, between 1977 and the mid-1980s, all murder convictions occurring in a district court, when appealed, were moved directly onto the Kansas Supreme Court's dockets, bypassing the newly formed Court of Appeals.

They considered Nelms, Myrick and Swain all indigent defendants, a person who has been charged with a crime but cannot afford to hire a lawyer due to lack of financial resources. Unlike today, the process of assigning attorneys to indigent defendants for appeals was different in the late 1970s. In 1982, the State of Kansas established the Kansas Appellate Defender Office (KADO), a centralized state agency staffed with attorneys specifically designated to handle appeals for indigent defendants.

Today, when a defendant files a notice of appeal, this office is typically assigned automatically to represent them. However, in 1978 and 1979, this system was not yet in place—particularly in serious cases like murder convictions—meaning indigent defendants had to rely on ad hoc appointments rather than a dedicated appellate defender.

After the convictions of Myrick and Nelms in Butler County District Court, both Myrick and Nelms filed a notice of appeal to Judge Benson through their attorneys White Jr. and Davis. Once Judge Benson received the notices of appeal, he then reassigned new attorneys for both Myrick and Nelms to handle their appeals from a list of local attorneys who were willing to handle appeals within the current appeals system.

Enter Attorney Olin Stansbury. Stansbury was the lucky attorney to draw the assignment of representing Myrick. Simply to make a somewhat boring portion of this story easier to get through,

I am going to tell you primarily about Myrick's appeal. Actually, Myrick had some arguable points to make, while Nelms really did not. It was mainly Myrick who appealed everything; however, Nelms threw in his two cents worth for an appeal as well.

In Myrick's case, they appealed his conviction, listing an array of issues he felt were grounds for a new trial. Myrick felt his attorney, and the system had cheated him, in addition to all the earlier issues he had raised during the trial that the judge had overruled. Attorney Stansbury began his fight on this client's behalf. Stansbury was an attorney in private practice at his own law firm in El Dorado, Kansas. Because he had not been involved, he did not know what had taken place at the trial.

Some defense attorneys may believe their clients are innocent or overcharged; however, if a defense attorney is honest with themselves, they would probably agree the percentage of completely innocent clients is quite low. Most defense attorneys simply have a job to do, and they will do it as vigorously as possible until they have burned up all their fuel and have run out of gas with no more legal options to pursue.

Defense attorney Stansbury was the latter, a hardworking attorney, who, once assigned to a client, worked to find closure for his client. Far from lazy or ineffective—he was a fighter and would do everything in his power that the law would allow.

Stansbury visited Myrick on several occasions in late 1978 and early 1979 at the Lansing Correctional Prison. He stayed for several hours during each visit. Stansbury, not having the knowledge from the trial, was starting fresh with his new client. He soon became prepared for a vigorous defense appeal.

During these interviews, Myrick told Stansbury many negative points about his trial and about his former assigned attorney White Jr. Myrick felt his first trial attorney, Doyle White Jr. 1: disliked him; 2: was unfair to him; 3: aided the prosecution, leading to a guilty verdict; 4: was biased due to personal friendships with Kansas Highway Patrol Troopers. Myrick displayed bitterness towards everyone because he adamantly believed all involved had set him up. He made these statements clear during the interviews with his new attorney, Stansbury.

After conducting the interviews with Myrick, Stansbury had many questions he would seek the answers to, both from the court records and from attorney Doyle E. White Jr. himself.

On August 29, 1979, Stansbury submitted an affidavit as an exhibit to the Butler County District Court to file the appeal documents to the Kansas Supreme Court. This affidavit would become a vital document as the first step in the Kansas Supreme Court's acceptance or denial of the appeal. The affidavit illustrated Myrick's former attorney, Doyle White Jr., had provided ineffective counsel during his previous defense.

Whether Stansbury really felt this way is unknown. However, it was the avenue he chose to assist Myrick in this appeal. The affidavit was crafted in such a way as to make the reader see Myrick's trial in a different light than what the jury did. Although authored completely by Stansbury, the words were clearly coming from Myrick himself.

The affidavit was four pages long, with one full-page attachment. Nine distinct points of contention raised by Myrick highlighted the unfairness of his trial. The affidavit was the framework for a motion for a new trial.

The following is one of many allegations Myrick asked to be raised on his behalf:
> "That while Jimmie Nelms was testifying, he [Nelms]
> whispered under his breath that he had never killed a man before."

As a result of this allegation, Stansbury did some detective work to see if he could prove Nelms had made that statement. Had he done so, it could potentially lessen the culpability of his client's murder charge. Stansbury reached out to Rosalie Brenton, who had been one of the twelve jurors who convicted Myrick. Brenton denied ever having heard Nelms make the statement. Stansbury had asked the same question of Doyle White Jr., who also denied ever hearing Nelms utter those specific words.

Stansbury then reviewed the court transcript and found on

Volume IX, page 1266, the following questioning between Nelms, who was testifying, and Assistant County Attorney Steve Robison:

Q: Assistant County Attorney Steve Robison
A: *Jimmie Nelms*

Q: Why are you scared? You did not do anything?
A: *I hadn't killed a man before, and that's, that's [sic] what it basically was-what it was. Three (3) mans [sic] on the scene of a murder.*

Q: Why did not you just sit there?
A: *I did not think I could have.*

Q: Why not?
A: *For fear of my life.*

Q: What do you mean, 'for fear of your life.'
A: *Well, it stands to reason if you kill someone and you are out on the highway and I say you can't go nowhere in my car, you are not going to stay there with a body with me; you are not going to leave me there to testify against you; so therefore, my life was in jeopardy whether I leave you or you leave me.*

This actual testimony by Nelms was shocking or at least it should have been.

Stansbury's affidavit to the Supreme Court of Kansas stated the following legal opinion:

> I have been led to believe, and the matter can be proven, that Nelms' statement on line 22 of page 1266 'I hadn't killed a man before, and that's'—was sotto voce and a confession from the stand, and that the balance was an attempt by the defendant Nelms to explain away his statement when he realized what he had confessed.' 'Sotto voce is Latin, meaning in a quiet voice, as to not be overheard.' Also known as a sotto voce remark.

In his next allegation, Myrick and Stansbury implicate White Jr. of having a financial arrangement with Butler County Attorneys Norman Manley and Steve Robison to secure a conviction of Myrick. Stansbury quotes a letter Myrick had written to Judge Benson after the conviction when he writes, "...how much did you get out of it? I know Manley or someone make [sic] you a deal. Man, you are so wrong, but tell me why? I really want to know."

In this section of the affidavit written for Myrick, Stansbury outlined on March 5, 1979, an article appeared on the front page of *The El Dorado Times* with the headline in bold print "Lawyer helps organize Trooper organization." In this article, it stated the "trial attorney Doyle White Jr. was assisting in organizing an association of the Kansas Highway Patrol." This statement alone, if true, could indicate a severe conflict of interest. It would lend credibility to Myrick's theory, and place White Jr. in a question of ethics.

Stark claims were made that Judge Benson, Manley, and/or White Jr. had a financial arrangement regarding helping the state secure a conviction and alleging White Jr. was openly biased in favor of the Kansas Highway Patrol. Myrick's claims, if accurate, could support a claim of ineffective counsel and warrant a new trial.

In his appeal's attached affidavit, Stansbury stated he was drafting a detailed letter of questions for Doyle White Jr., hoping to help the court decide if White Jr. provided ineffective counsel. Attorney Stansbury wrote the following in a certified letter sent to White Jr.'s law firm:

> You are entitled to the understanding of the manner in which these issues were brought to my attention:
>
> quote from the letter you received from Myrick dated November 16, 1978: ... 'You've helped Manley and that other DA convict me...to set me up...' To which Myrick in my questioning 03/22/79 explained, "It's obvious the man did not defend me...like from the closing statement of the trial...He told the jury in so many ways that he wanted to see me in prison.

Similar comments were made in his letter to the District Judge requesting a change of counsel. These were: 'Myrick contends he lost faith in you from the beginning.' One of his principal objections seems to be that in your initial contact, 'you told him he'd be going to prison before you let him tell his side of the [sic] things.'

Myrick contends you helped 'Manley and the other DA work out some problem to help convict him during a trial recess. This was in the judge's chambers in the absence of the Judge, Nelms and Mr. Davis. The subject matter apparently referred to reversal of trial or something...when you pointed out what they were doing wrong...'he was actually showing them what they were doing wrong'...he was helping the DA.

Myrick felt you were too friendly with the opposition in general. He felt he did not have a chance because he did not have anybody representing him. He admitted you advised him to take the stand. "Let's say to a certain degree he did"' I asked why he did not follow your advice. He said, "it still wouldn't have done any good... cause I still would have to go to prison for life...because people already had in their minds what they were going to do... It was written all over their faces...Hatred in their eyes.

He seemed to blame you for the sheriff's officers wrestling him to the floor in the jail during trial days to cut off his fingernails at your direction.

Several months ago, you mentioned something to the effect that the preparation for trial and the trial itself had left you mentally exhausted, that you had feelings of futility, had experienced 'emotional drain,' and that your relationship with former friends in law enforcement seemed to have changed. As a consequence of that statement, your known history as a former county attorney and an associate of police personnel as evidenced in your publicized organization of a state highway patrol association, I find myself obliged to inquire on Myrick's behalf and to the facts as you know them on certain issues, including your prior representation of any clients who might have been witnesses against Myrick or his co-defendants.

Stansbury asked Doyle White Jr. to respond to the following questions:

> Considering the above, I would appreciate your reply to the following questions to the extent that you feel free to do so. Concerning a conflict of interest:
>
>> During the year immediately preceding your appointment as Myrick's counsel, did you represent any members (or family members) of the El Dorado Public Safety Department, The Butler County Sheriff's Department or the Kansas Highway Patrol who had any direct connection to this case as it evolved?
>>
>> Did you represent any other such person during your representation of Myrick?
>> Without invading any rights of those clients, will you please describe as best you can their relationship to this case and the general representation of them?
>>
>> During your representation of Myrick, which, if any, of the above might be considered by you to be 'continuing clients,' which I might define as those whom you would expect to look to you for legal advice either during or after your representation

of Myrick?

Had you taken any part in the organization of the Highway Patrolmen's association before or during your representation of Myrick? May I have the date of your first involvement?

Stansbury wanted answers to this last question. It was this answer, which could open the way for him to push forward into building his grounds for a new trial. It did not appear Stansbury wished to expose or damage White Jr.'s reputation. He simply needed an avenue to use to reach his goal for Myrick.

The questionnaire within the letter continued...

Do you have any information other than may appear on the transcript relative to the following?

The reason for the heavy protection of the courtroom?

The parking of 6 to 8 highway patrol or sheriff's department vehicles immediately in front of the judicial building during the trial?

The presence of armed guards both inside and outside the building during the preliminary hearing and the trial?

Handcuffs on Mr. Myrick in the presence of the jury?*

Mr. Myrick's appearance in court for trial wearing prison coveralls, socks and shower shoes?

How many uniformed peace officers appeared in the courtroom during trial from day to day? How many were there who had not been called as witnesses?

*Under the 2025 judicial system, this alone would warrant a mistrial.

Sheriff's officers (on your instruction) manhandling Myrick to clip his fingernails at the end of one trial day?

Did you appear on an area television broadcast after the trial in which you stated that you believed Myrick received a fair trial? Please comment.

In your closing argument, did you actually say words to the effect that you 'were mad about the incident and had a bad attitude toward your client?

Is there something in this case known to you that dictated Myrick's decision not to testify? If so, what?

Can you explain any situation during trial recess that Myrick might have misinterpreted as your helping the 'DA convict him?'

Can you recall your initial contact with Myrick? If so, when was this? Did you tell him he was going to go to prison before he even discussed the facts as he knew them?"

Do you believe you were in any way not capable of carrying through with Myrick's defense due to exhaustion, outside pressure or otherwise?

Stansbury ended the letter to Doyle White Jr. by stating:

> Thank you very much for your kind assistance in resolving the issues in this matter.
> Sincerely yours, Olin Stansbury.

15: THE REPLY

On May 3, 1979, Attorney Doyle White Jr. replied in writing to Stansbury's questions. A hint of discontent colored his otherwise professional answers. Suffice it to say, Doyle White Jr. was pissed about having to answer for his earlier appointed service to Walter Myrick.

The letter written by Doyle White Jr. began: "REPLY OF TRIAL COUNSEL TO APPELLANT COUNSEL."

In repeating the exact questions from Stansbury, it read:

Dear Olin:
Directing your attention to the questions you have propounded in your letter dated April 24, 1979:
Concerning a conflict of interest:

During the year immediately preceding your appointment as Myrick's counsel, did you represent any members (or family members) of the El Dorado Public Safety Department, The Butler County Sheriff's Department or the Kansas Highway Patrol who had any direct connection to this case as it evolved?
Answer: Yes.

[Note: However, Doyle White Jr. does not give any details regarding who he represented or if the contacts would constitute a conflict.]

Did you represent any other such person during your representation of Myrick?
Answer: No. Without invading any rights of those and the general representation of them?

During your representation of Myrick, which, if any, of the above might be considered by you to be 'continuing clients' which, I might define as those whom you would expect to look to you for legal advice either during or after your representation of Myrick?
Answer: All, I suppose, subject to their vagarities.

Continuation of Doyle White, Jr's reply:

Had you taken any part in the organization of the Highway Patrolmen's association before or during your representation of Myrick? May I have the date of your first involvement?
Answer: Approximately six months before I was appointed to represent Walter Myrick, I talked with two troopers about the formation of an association. I did not talk to anyone about the association again until approximately three months ago.

Do you have any information other than may appear on the transcript relative to the following:?
The reason for the heavy protection of the courtroom?
Answer: No.

The parking of 6 to 8 highway patrol or sheriff's department vehicles immediately in front of the judicial building during the trial?
Answer: No.

The presence of armed guards both inside and outside the building during the preliminary hearing and the trial?
Answer: No.

Handcuffs on Mr. Myrick in the presence of the jury?
Answer: "No."

Mr. Myrick's appearance in court for trial wearing prison coveralls, socks and shower shoes?
Answer: He had no other clothing and did not desire me to secure other clothing.

How many uniformed peace officers appeared in the courtroom during trial from day to day? How many were there who had not been called as witnesses?
Answer: I don't remember.

Continuation of Doyle White, Jr's reply:

>Sheriff's officers (on your instruction) manhandling Myrick to clip his fingernails at the end of one trial day?
>*Answer: I did not instruct the sheriff's officers to clip Mr. Myrick's fingernails. I had requested him to do so because I thought it would improve his appearance. I was told by Ron Peters that he felt the long fingernails posed a security problem and when Mr. Myrick refused to cut them, Peters cut them for him.*
>
>Did you appear on an area television broadcast after the trial in which you stated that you believed Myrick received a fair trial?
>*Answer: Yes, no comment necessary.*
>
>In your closing argument, did you actually say words to the effect that you "were mad about the incident and had a bad attitude toward your client?
>Answer: No, please refer to the transcript.
>Is there something in this case known to you that dictated Myrick's decision not to testify?
>*Answer: Nothing 'dictated' Myrick's decision not to testify. He made it on his own free will.*
>
>Can you explained [sic] any situation during trial recess that Myrick might have misinterpreted as your helping the 'DA convict him.'
>Answer: No.
>
>Can you recall your initial contact with Myrick? If so, when was this? Did you tell him he was going to go to prison before he even discussed the facts as he knew them?
>*Answer: I recall graphically my initial contact with Mr. Myrick, I don't remember the date, but it was the date he was brought to Butler County. I told him there was a substantial chance that no matter what the facts really were he would spend a considerable time in prison.*

Continuation of Doyle White, Jr's reply:

> Do you believe you were in any way not capable of carrying through with Myrick's defense due to exhaustion, outside pressure or otherwise?
> ***Answer: Of course not. I was in excellent physical and emotional condition and did an outstanding job for my client.***
> ***Signed: Very truly yours, Doyle White Jr.***

From the answers Doyle White Jr. gave, one could assert that he did not appreciate the manner of questioning, or his abilities or effort being questioned in this case. It was obvious, he wished he had never been assigned the case or ever met Walter Myrick.

The affidavit drafted by Olin Stansbury, along with the response letter by Doyle White Jr. would be submitted by Olin to the Kansas Supreme Court, along with an affidavit authored by Walter Myrick entitled "Walter Myrick's story."

The affidavit began with Myrick's incensed rebuke of his trial counsel, Doyle White Jr. showing several examples of how he saw the proceedings against him as being unfair and ineffective. After showing his disgust for his trial counsel, he gave a written statement as to what occurred on May 24, 1978, at Matfield Green. It was a confession of sorts, as well as his request for freedom, all spelled out for the courts to read. Had Myrick testified at the trial with the same or similar statements as he had written in this affidavit, it may have actually helped him. His testimony may have given him at least a chance of being convicted of a lesser charge.

16: WALTER MYRICK'S STORY

On August 22, 1979, Walter Myrick authored an affidavit titled:
EXHIBIT E.
DEFENDANTS AFFIDAVIT

The following is a portion of what Walter Myrick told the court:

> I believe I had a good defense to the charges that were made against me, and had I had an attorney who was willing to properly defend me, I would have been acquitted. In support of that, I would have testified at trial as follows:
>
> I was stopped for speeding and was asked to accompany the patrolman back to his patrol car and was sitting in the patrol car while he filled out a ticket when Nelms came back to the driver's window and threw a gun down on the patrolman. Before he pulled a gun, he asked the patrolman, 'What was the trouble?' The patrolman said he was going to have to give me a ticket for driving without a license.
>
> As the patrolman was saying this, Nelms was getting himself into a position where he could get the drop on the patrolman. I did not have time to think or yell a warning. The next thing I knew, he had a gun on him. It was just that simple and fast. Altogether, the whole thing did not take more than three to five minutes. The whole time we were there. After pulling the gun on the patrolman, Nelms said 'put your hands up, put your hands up on top of your head,' because the Trooper did not have his hat on. Then the Trooper tried to move. I don't know what happened to me, but I know the Patrolman was panicked and Nelms made him step out of the car and keep his hands up. Then Nelms took the patrolman's gun and stuck it in the front of his waistband.

Continuation of Walter Myrick's testimony in court:

> When he got out, he walked him around behind the car and I got out and said to Nelms 'What...what you gonna do, man?' Nelms did not said [sic] anything, so I said again, 'What are you going to do, man?' Nelms still did not said [sic] anything. The Trooper kept trying to lay [sic] on, trying to lower his hands. I say [sic] he must have had another gun with him, but Nelms still did not answer me. All the time, I'm following him because I'm curious so I said a third time 'What are you gonna do?' He still did not answere [sic] me. He really had to pay attention to this man, because the man kept trying to ease, trying to take his hands off his head, trying to get to what must have been a gun. So we walked, I don't know how far we walked, then Nelms hit him over the head with the barrel of his gun. The officer fell first to his knees and then fell flat out [sic] on his face, and I said 'they're out of their minds.' Even after that happened I think that's the end of it cause he was just going to hit him over the head and then get in the car and escape.
>
> In just seconds Nelms fired two bullets and ran for the car. I was totally stunned and in a state of shock. I am standing somewhere close to the patrolman. I don't even remember going completely down in the ditch with him, but I might have. I understand that my footprints were found close around the patrolman's body. I might have even gone down to see if there was anything to do to help. The whole incident happened so fast that I found myself standing there abandoned as Nelms ran for the driver's door of the car. I ran for the car and jumped in the back seat.
>
> Nelms sent Swain back to the patrol car and told him to take a towel we had in the car and wipe up Nelms' fingerprints. Swain went back to the car, and we left when he returned.

> I really don't know anything about what happened from then, until I found us making a U-turn in a pasture heading back for what appeared to be a policeman's car. There was testimony that I shot at the patrolman. [*referring to Trooper Charlie Smith.*] That is not correct. I never fired a single shot. After the shooting incident began, Nelms had apparently fired all the shells in one gun and threw it back to me. He turned around, waved his gun at me and said, 'man help me.' I thought he was going to shoot me if I did not do something, so I moved to the right rear window, rolled it down, and stuck what I thought was an empty gun out the window, but I never fired it.

This last statement matches what Trooper Charlie Smith said Myrick had done during the shootout.

Myrick continues his statement:

> I was of the opinion to the extent that I could do any thinking at all due to the shock of the killing that I would be killed by the police for what Nelms had done if they caught him with me, and I made an effort to run and escape to save my life. After we were captured, I was taken to a [*sic*] Chief Woody's patrol car where he read me my rights and told me I had a right to talk to an attorney before I said anything to him. I told him I would like to talk to a lawyer. Then he told me a lawyer wouldn't do me no [*sic*] good, that my best shot would be to talk to him. He persisted in asking me questions about what was going on, and I think I told him we were on our way to where we were going. He said we had really gotten lost and he started questioning me about the Trooper, and I was so afraid he or someone else on the police force would kill me, that I denied knowing anything about the killing of the Trooper.

Continuation of Walter Myrick's testimony in court:

> About that time Swain was being brought in and he was already talking to police officers, telling them all about things. They brought Swain up to the car I was in and I asked him what he was going to do and he said he was not going to take a murder rap for nobody, he wouldn't take a murder rap for his momma, and that we should tell the police that Nelms did it.

Walter Myrick ended this portion of his affidavit by saying:

> I did not know anything about planning or premeditating any murder: I did not help Nelms in any way other than trying to get away before someone, Nelms or the police shot me. I did not kidnap the patrolman; and I did not have any gun until Nelms threw the empty gun at me at Herington.

Myrick signed the affidavit, and a notary public notarized it. Although some, if not most, of Myrick's affidavit is very possibly true, there are portions of what happened, which Myrick either left out or simply forgot to mention. According to Swain, Myrick had discarded the ticket book and the Smith and Wesson handgun stolen from Conroy O'Brien by throwing them out the window during the chase with Trooper Charlie Smith. These facts, which make it look as if he was trying to conceal evidence, must have slipped his mind.

Swain was adamant that Myrick had thrown the ticket book out of the car as they were fleeing the murder scene. It was also Myrick who had thrown Conroy's revolver out near the Dickinson County line, and it had been Swain who had shown the investigators the locations where they were later found. Both Swain and Myrick also swore under oath that "it had been Nelms who kidnapped and killed Conroy," Swain by testimony and Myrick through his affidavit.

Neither of their stories ever changed from their original versions.

So, did any of this matter regarding Walter Myrick being given a new trial by the Kansas Supreme Court? The answer is no—no it did not.

The higher court reached the same conclusion on all the issues raised on appeal. Judge Benson had made no errors on any of his rulings, and all arguments were without merit.

The life sentences for both Nelms and Myrick for first degree murder, aggravated kidnapping and unlawful use of a firearm by a convicted felon would stand.

Although Walter Myrick had not actually pulled the trigger or killed Conroy O'Brien, the fact remains he was present with Nelms. Swain accepted a plea deal, resulting in a conviction on reduced charges.

The court saw Myrick was a willing criminal partner to Nelms and had done nothing to stop the killing when he had the opportunity, nor did he ever attempt or persuade Nelms to stop.

The court decided their opinion of Myrick's culpability by stating "Walter Myrick was such a criminal partner of Nelms' that he had reached a handgun out the window of a moving car and pointed it at Trooper Charlie Smith, while Nelms fired upon Trooper Smith."

Had Myrick testified at his trial, the jury might have diminished some of his culpability, and they might have sided with him on the murder charge, but this did not happen. The jury determined he was just as guilty as Nelms, and he was going to pay the same price.

17: THE PRISON SENTENCES

Each of the suspects in the murder of Trooper Conroy O'Brien had committed crimes that the State of Kansas had charged and they believed were appropriate.

Giving Swain a plea deal did not bother Norman Manley, nor the court.

Stanford Swain was twenty-one years old at the time and, in the eyes of the state, was less culpable of the three men initially charged with Conroy's death. Swain had remained inside of the Mercury during the murder, although he too had done nothing to stop the act of murder. Swain had followed an order or request given by Nelms, and it is believed Swain alone would not have initiated the murder or helped in it.

Swain did not take part in any portion of the shootout with Trooper Charlie Smith and had actually fled at the first instance he could have. Swain was the first of the suspects to give any details to the police about what had occurred at Matfield Green, and he had not tried to minimize his role in any of it. Swain was allowed to plead to the charges of aiding a felon and unlawful possession of a firearm. On August 15, 1978, the court gave him a prison sentence of six to twenty years. Swain would serve ten years in prison, and then they paroled him back to his home state of Oklahoma on July 6, 1988.

This parole by the Kansas Department of Corrections of releasing Swain into the state of Oklahoma would later infuriate both Tanda O'Brien and her daughter, Neely. More than the freedom granted to Swain, their concern was the Kansas Department of Corrections failed to notify them about his release into their home state, where they had lived since 1990.

At both Nelms and Myrick's sentencings, the state's lead attorney, Norman Manley, asked the court, "to give both Nelms and Myrick the absolute maximum sentence possible." Manley told the court, "since we cannot hang them with the same rope, we can at least give them the same life sentences." Judge Benson agreed.

For Walter Myrick, his conviction for first-degree murder, unlawful possession of a firearm and aggravated kidnapping would, in a sense, end up being a death sentence for him. Myrick, sentenced to two life terms in prison beginning September 19, 1978, would serve the sentence entirely at the Lansing Correctional Facility, until his death on March 16, 2009. Myrick stood in front of the parole board many times during his thirty years in prison, and the parole board always rejected his request for parole.

For Nelms, his fate would be similar to Walter Myrick's, it would just take longer. Judge Benson gave him the same two life terms for first-degree murder, aggravated kidnaping, and unlawful weapons charges as he had for Myrick. During his incarceration, Nelms visited every prison the state of Kansas had available. Nelms served time at the Lansing Correctional Facility, Hutchinson Correctional Facility, El Dorado Correctional Facility, Larned Correctional Mental Facility, Norton Correctional Facility, finally ending up serving his last days to date at the medium security prison at the Winfield Correctional Facility.

The Kansas Parole Board, composed of three representatives, held a parole hearing via Zoom (video conferencing), on May 1, 2025. After collecting information during the meeting, the board actually issued Nelms' parole, which set his release for August 2025. Because of the possibility of parole, Nelms had planned to live with his elderly sister in the Dallas, Texas, area.

Only the people close to Nelms, who are on his approved visitation list, can speak with him, so his true feelings regarding his parole are unknown.

News of Nelms' parole spread rapidly across Kansas via email, television and newspapers on May 7, 2025. KWCH 12 News in Wichita, began investigating the parole and in doing so, contacted Trooper Charlie Smith's daughter. Charlie has since passed away, but his children have never forgotten the day Nelms tried killing their dad.

On the evening news, Trooper Smith's daughter, Brenda, spoke of how horrified and scared she was for Nelms to be released. She spoke of how Nelms had come very close to killing her father and how unjust the parole of Nelms was to every citizen in Kansas. The interview with Brenda was heartfelt, conjuring emotions in everyone who was associated with this case.

Many voices spoke up to tell the parole board and Kansas

Governor Laura Kelly how they felt. The people who spoke up were not happy with the parole board and let it be known how the entire state of Kansas felt about their unjust decision to release Nelms. These voices included many citizens, including the family of Conroy O'Brien and the children of Charlie Smith, the Kansas Troopers Association, and the Colonel of the Highway Patrol. This vocal resistance sparked a debate in Topeka, Kansas.

More than likely, it had been Governor Laura Kelly who led the decision that would soon follow. On May 13, 2025, as a result of the public outcry, a news outlet reported that the Kansas Parole Board was rescinding their offer of parole to Nelms, making his next chance at parole scheduled for May 1, 2027.

By 2027, Nelms will have served more than forty-nine years in prison.

Jimmie K. Nelms   Walter Myrick   Stanford Swain

Images from public files. Kansas Department of Corrections.

18: CONTACT WITH A MURDERER

On at least three occasions in 2010, Nelms corresponded with Conroy's daughter, Neely O'Brien-Goen, through letters he had written to her. In these letters, Nelms thanked Neely for forgiving him, and he claimed to have found the Lord. Nelms told Neely that he had begun making jewelry while in prison and wished to send her some for her and her children to enjoy. After receiving the jewelry, Nelms' correspondence stopped for whatever reason, and Neely has not heard from him in the past fifteen years. To date (2025), Nelms has served forty-seven years in prison for killing Conroy O'Brien. At least seven times the parole board considered him for parole, but they denied it each time. Each parole hearing is like a fresh cut to the heart of Conroy's family members, as if each parole notification reopens the scars of deep wounds.

Tanda has attended many of the hearings and hopes Nelms remains in prison for the rest of his life. She spoke to Nelms during one of his hearings and has nothing else to say to him or the parole board. As a result, she will not be attending any hearings in the future.

Neely attended her final hearing when she was twenty years old. When given the opportunity to be heard, Neely informed the parole board she had forgiven Nelms and, in doing so, had allowed herself to heal and free her heart from the burden of anger and hatred. Neely believes whatever decision the parole board makes about Nelms' fate is fine with her. She has found peace in the entire situation.

However, Tanda has never forgiven Nelms and is hopeful he lives his remaining days in prison, paying for his crime, which robbed her of a wonderful husband and the father of her child. Tanda has not found true peace since May 24, 1978, and believes she may never find it again, at least not as long as Nelms is on this earth.

A side note regarding the Mercury car: The KBI (Kansas Bureau of Investigation) processed the 1973 Mercury Marquis owned by Laddie Meeks, which had been crashed and severely damaged, and later towed to Baxter Construction Company. It remained in storage for over one year. By June 1979, investigators had been unable to contact Meeks. Nor had Meeks made any attempt to get his car returned. The reason there was no attempt was because after loaning his car to Myrick, Meeks was arrested in Carroll County, Mississippi, for shooting into an occupied dwelling after a drug deal went wrong. Meeks was unavailable to locate or retrieve the car, and due to his own legal matters, may have written it off as a loss. Meeks found himself being sentenced to serve a five-year prison term in Mississippi for this conviction.

As a result, Dickinson County Sheriff Jim McKenney obtained the legal paperwork to have the car sold at a public auction to recoup some of the money owed to the wrecker service.

Sheriff McKenney completed the sheriff's auction; however, no bidders placed a bid that would satisfy the $1,143.60 owed to Baxter Construction Company for towing and storage. Sheriff McKenney then awarded the car to Kenneth Baxter, who became the proud owner of this quasi-famous car.

Kenneth Baxter kept the car outside for a period of time for people to come and gawk at, proclaiming it as "being the car involved in a murder and famous shoot-out by the Highway Patrol." The Mercury's final resting place is unknown.

19: THE HIGHWAY

Driving north out of Abbyville, Kansas, on Hodge Road leads you to travel on a nicely maintained sand and gravel country road. The Abbyville cemetery sits on a two-acre plot along the west edge of Hodge Road, with three narrow entrances to pass through. In the northwest corner of the cemetery is a beautiful black headstone surrounded by displays of loving affection, left by friends and family during the most recent memorial weekend.

The front of the headstone will forever display the name CONROY G. O'BRIEN, flanked on both sides by engravings of a six-pointed Kansas Highway Patrol badge.

The back of the stone displays a large engraving of the Kansas Highway Patrol badge for all to see. His epitaph reads:

> Loving Husband & Public Servant,
> Made Supreme Sacrifice in the Line of Duty, leaving behind many memories of himself to his fellow law enforcement officers and family.

As you leave the cemetery and turn north, you find what was once US Route-50, one half mile to the north. The highway, now named Trooper Conroy G. O'Brien Memorial Highway, runs from US Route-61, northwest for over 50 miles, to the city limits of Sylvia, Kansas. This section of highway, memorializing Trooper Conroy O'Brien, became official through the passing of Kansas House Bill 2581, signed on July 1, 2018, by Governor Jeff Colyer.

Conroy O'Brien's memory lives on through his family and friends, who will never forget the sacrifice he made to the great state of Kansas. May he rest in peace.

Conroy O'Brien Memorial Highway, taken by author, Jim Norton, 2024.

20: A FATHER'S LOVE

Early in Tanda's pregnancy, when the spotting and hemorrhaging began, she was not sure if she would be able to give Conroy the perfect gift he so desired. This unknowingly left her with a sense of dread that could never be cleansed, or so she thought. Take, for instance, the death of a loved one. A truly respected state trooper who was so full of life. How is anyone to explain his death other than to say it was tragic, unnecessary, and heart wrenching? Yes, it was all of those things. However, to Tanda, it may have also been something else. For the two ladies so closely involved in his life and his story, their truth resonates deeply within each of them, to this day. A belief that God Himself played a huge part in the whole thing. Tanda and Neely each share their deeply held beliefs that the Lord, in his own way, had intervened. God simply traded the soul of Conroy O'Brien for the life and living soul of his daughter, Neely. Neely believes in her heart that, had Conroy not died, she would not have been born healthy.

Neely and Tanda both have an explanation for this belief. According to Tanda, "all at once my health issues, which so dangerously threatened the pregnancy, simply and silently vanished when Conroy was taken from me." Some coincidences are unable to be explained and should not be overlooked, when you examine everything through their eyes.

Tanda, while sitting at her dinner table, quietly explained, "When Conroy died, both of his hands were lying on the top of his head and when Neely was born, she came into the world with both her hands lying on top of her head." As strong as any conviction can be, Neely and Tanda both believe in their hearts that God traded Conroy for Neely.

Over the years, Neely has pondered her father and his death many times. Once, as she sat in deep thought, a twelve-year-old Neely experienced a moment so profound it changed her forever. As this moment of clarity came over her, Neely witnessed a conversation taking place between Jesus and her dad. As she sat frozen in her thoughts, she saw Jesus and Conroy sitting on the trunk lid of his patrol car, chatting. Neely could hear Jesus say to her dad, "It will be okay now, Conroy." For Neely, her dad's death was absolutely an exchange. A trade, if you will. A trade which allowed his daughter to be born and live in peace. There is no love, such as the love between a father and his daughter.

Message left by Neely on her dad's End of Watch message board. Father for the sacrifice that you made to the state of Kansas...Thank you. I know that I never got to meet you in person, but I know that you are with me all the time and have been from the beginning. Out of a tragedy rose miraculous blessings...May God remind me daily, to never take for granted the price you paid. I love you.

Neely Mayree O'Brien-Goen
Daughter
October 29, 2006

AFTERWORD

Afterword by the Author

I wrote this book as a tribute to a man I had never met. Someone who holds a special place for so many people. A friend once asked me why I wanted to tell stories such as Conroy's or Jerry Ivey's. I guess it is because I believe these stories and many more need to be told.

As for my earlier connection to Trooper Charlie Smith and the Kansas Highway Patrol, through my father, Sergeant Bobby Lee Norton, I simply felt drawn to write about the hero who is Trooper Conroy O'Brien.

This story's journey began when I reached out to Neely O'Brien-Goen, who I am certain was shocked that I inquired about her long-lost father. Neely agreed to speak with her mother about my idea of writing Conroy's story, and Tanda was gracious enough to give me her permission.

In early December 2024, as I was preparing to conduct research for the book, I drove south to meet with Tanda and Neely. I had learned all I could through the internet, and it was time to speak to the people who really mattered. What I found was a charming widow and her intelligent daughter. Sitting at Tanda's dining table, I felt as if I were sitting amongst royalty. I was speaking with a woman who had endured something so heartbreaking and unimaginable. Tanda was more than willing to open herself to answering my questions to accomplish my goal of telling Conroy's story. Tanda detailed her early life of love and loss, from dating to the fateful day she lost Conroy. It brought back a flood of emotions for her. However, she never wavered as she described her life with Conrcy. Tanda gave all the details I would need to tell of their personal lives, the love and the journey, which ended way too soon.

I am grateful and full of admiration for Tanda. I feel I am a better person after getting to know her. Conroy's daughter, Neely, although unable to tell specifics about her dad, gave insight only a daughter could give. Neely knows she is here because of her hero father, and her spirituality shines through when she speaks of Conroy. I hope I conveyed their love of Conroy throughout this book.

As for my knowledge of Trooper Charlie Smith, I am blessed for ever getting to know the man. My father gave me this opportunity. An opportunity only a cop's kid could get to experience.

What I hope readers take away from Murder at Matfield Green is the tragic legacy of someone who blessed so many, and a memory of a man who has been immortalized by his community and friends.

Losing a police officer in the line of duty is something few citizens actually understand or dwell on. The depth of sadness, sorrow and loss felt by the families, which include husbands, wives, sons, daughters and friends, is unimaginable. Conroy's death caused deep emotional scars to everyone who knew him, and are still felt to this day.

Conroy has had a highway named in his honor, and you cannot travel through Abbyville, Kansas, without seeing his image. He was a good man, a good friend and a good Kansas State Trooper.

Although the man who killed him has served over 47 years of his life behind bars for his crime, his life was also altered and basically destroyed on May 24, 1978 as well. Nelms was a hardened criminal, and his punishment has cost him his freedom through his 30s, 40s, 50s, 60s and 70s. I have wondered how he actually feels about his actions on that fateful day. I would hope, knowing what he knows now, that he would have stayed inside the Mercury and left Conroy to do his job.

Author, Jim Norton
Gold Badge Writing

ACKNOWLEDGMENTS & SOURCES

I'm deeply grateful to everyone who lent their support in the creation of Conroy's book; their contributions were invaluable. Their insights, the stories they recounted, their teamwork, and the practical help they offered proved absolutely critical; I could not have succeeded otherwise.

Tanda O'Brien Ulm: Conroy's widow and a wonderful lady. Thank you for your time and the insight you gave to me. Conroy was lucky to have you.

Neely (O'Brien) Goen: Conroy's daughter, who was not fortunate to have ever met her father. Neely, thank you for your time and details and the feelings you shared. Conroy smiles down on you daily. He is very proud of you.

Trooper Tony VanBuren (retired): Your memory is better than you think it is. Thank you for the details you remembered.

Trooper Nate Sparks (retired): Thank you for all your help in getting the details of the arrests and Charlie's shootout correct.

Trooper Mick Allen (retired): Mick, thank you for the information you gave. It was very helpful.

Jenny Knoche: Fairfield School District. Thank you for the details you could provide about Conroy's schooling and the scholarship program you help with. I hope you include this book along with the scholarships.

Jim Strong: Conroy's lifelong friend. Thank you for sharing your time and sharing about your childhood with Conroy.

Doyle Eiling: Conroy's lifelong friend. Thank you for sharing your time and sharing about your childhood with Conroy.

The Butler County, Kansas, Clerk of the District Court and office personnel: Thank you for the hundreds of court documents you copied and shared with me. These documents were beneficial in helping to clarify the details in the court cases.

Sterling College—Scott Downing and staff: Thank you for the information about Conroy's early college days and the photos you allowed me to use in the book.

Andy Meek: My friend and trusted beta reader for this manuscript. You do not know how much I appreciate all of your information, criticism and thoughts that make the book so much better.

Tim Wilkins: My nephew, who line edited the manuscript and gave me the needed English perfection, he gave.

Amy Norton: My wife, for your brilliance and assistance with the legal issues in this case, and for looking at the manuscript with the view I needed. I love you.

Jennifer Toelle: My publisher, proofer, editor, cover designer and friend. Thank you for your patience and everything you have poured into this project. Including biographical research assistance on Conroy's parents.

Springfield, Missouri, Police Department Records Division—Clerk Karen Ostby: Thank you for sharing the report and details of the Fugitt-Guin jewelry store robbery.

Kansas Bureau of Investigation, Director Tony Mattivi: Thank you for your help in getting the case file, which helped ensure accuracy within this story. You and your time are greatly appreciated.

And lastly, **Stanford Swain.** Yes, that Stanford Swain. I reached out to Swain and asked him if he would be willing to speak about the ordeal and how it changed his life. Swain is now an older man, who has lived a hard life. He spent years in prison and is now a free man. Swain, thank you for being honest with me and helping me fill in some empty spots. While Swain was not completely comfortable reliving the ordeal, he did answer a few questions, which did help.

The author conducted the research for this book using historical newspaper articles, affidavits, court documents, police reports and interviews with people who were involved with the investigations or with Conroy O'Brien personally.

Doing the research for this book was an eye-opening journey. I feel grateful to have researched and written it. Conroy's story needed to be shared with the world.

About the Author

Jim Norton, a retired police officer with 29 years of experience, is a dedicated true crime writer who conducts his own in-depth research. As the founder of Gold Badge Writing, he brings real-world insight to his storytelling. Jim lives in Central Kansas.

www.ingramcontent.com/pod-product-compliance
Lightning Source LLC
Chambersburg PA
CBHW060503030426
42337CB00015B/1710